The ESR Story: 1985–2010

By Eileen R. Kinch

EARLHAM
SCHOOL *of* RELIGION

Richmond, Indiana

50th Anniversary Volume

To Ruthann
Many blessings.
Faithfully,
Eileen R. Kinch

The ESR Story: 1985–2010

Cover design: Tim Seid

Library of Congress Cataloging-In-Publication Data

Kinch, Eileen R., 1981–
The ESR Story: 1985–2010
ISBN 978-1-879117-21-1

1. Religion   2. Quakerism

2009931726

We hold that Christ is present,
guiding and
directing our lives,
and that we can
know and obey
Christ's will.

TABLE OF CONTENTS

ACKNOWLEDGMENTS

This book is the result of help and input from many people. Thanks go to Friends Collection and Archives staff: Tom Hamm, Anne Thomason, and Michelle Riggs; to Bethany-related folks: Murray Wagner, Eugene Roop, Wayne Miller, and Ruthann Knechel Johansen; and a whole host of ESR and Earlham College-related people: Andy and Dorothy Grannell and Phyllis Wetherell; Doug Bennett, Dick Smith, Jay Marshall, Tom Mullen, Alan Kolp, Sue Kern, and Keith Esch; John and Ann Miller; Ken and Katharine Jacobsen; David Johns, Stephanie Crumley-Effinger, Lonnie Valentine, and Joanna Schofield; Suzanne LeVesconte, Mike Fales, Donne Hayden, Derek Parker, and John Punshon. Thanks also to Earlham Press.

Thanks to all those who granted interviews, answered questions via e-mail, located documents, and corrected my understanding.

Special thanks go to Jay Marshall and Donna Trankley, for arrangements, fact-checking, and guidance; Michael McCully, for editorial advice and encouragement; Louise Beede, for gracious and generous hospitality; and Keystone Fellowship Meeting and Michael, Marie, and Joanne Riegle Kinch, for just about everything else.

In Commemoration of Thomas J. Mullen

Eileen Kinch's fine recounting of ESR's second 25 years pays tribute to the many personalities who contributed to the life and progress of the institution. As this written history neared completion, word arrived that Tom Mullen had died of a massive stroke at the age of 74. Tom joined the School of Religion as Lecturer in 1966, later becoming a professor of Applied Theology. Following Wil Cooper and Alan Kolp, he assumed the deanship in 1984. Without question, Tom was a key figure during the school's quarter of a century. His contributions to ESR were many; three in particular left indelible impressions on the school.

Tom Mullen had the delightful gift of finding humor in nearly every facet of life. One of my earliest encounters with him was during one of his hospital stays. Within two minutes of my arrival, he quipped that his colostomy would complicate his life, as it would be difficult to find shoes to match his bag. Tom unleashed that treasured gift of humor as he taught students the details of practical, in-the-trenches acts of ministry. It permeated his preaching and writing as he offered wisdom to external audiences. It helped define his institutional presence as dean, allowing him to communicate effectively across Friends' broad spectrum so that ESR's mission and need could be heard by a larger audience. His gift of humor had a transformative effect on the classroom, worship, administration, and ultimately on lives.

Tom was also an outstanding fundraiser. As dean, he played a key role in the School of Religion's Make a Difference campaign, launched in 1986. The success of that campaign provided the necessary funds to construct the ESR Center and to renovate the Robert Barclay Center. Those projects were significant for the campus ethos. ESR originally occupied houses located on the Earlham campus. The construction of the ESR Center gave the seminary a distinct visibility that it had previously lacked, as it signified institutional permanence with a style reminiscent of historic Quaker meetinghouses. It is difficult to overestimate the importance of Tom's ability as a fundraiser in this effort.

Finally, Tom Mullen's ministry of writing has forever influenced ESR's educational program. Quakers have a long history of writing for various reasons. Tom's passion for and success in writing for the religious market provided the impetus for developing a curriculum devoted to the concept of writing as ministry. Friends of the school endowed a Ministry of Writing Colloquium to honor Tom when he retired as dean of the school. Later as a tribute to his younger brother, Frank Mullen endowed the Mullen Ministry of Writing Program. In effect, Tom's gift of writing allowed ESR to develop a program niche in the competitive field of theological education.

Each of us passes through life as a wrinkle in time. All lives are valuable, and some are particularly memorable. With *The ESR Story: 1985–2010*, we commemorate the life of one whose efforts we want to remember.

Jay Marshall
Dean of Earlham School of Religion

INTRODUCTION

The Paradox of the Quaker Ministry and ESR: Revisited

Fifty years ago, Elton Trueblood observed that Quaker ministry holds two seemingly contradictory truths. On the one hand, Quakers claim universal ministry, saying all men and women are called to be ministers, and Christ's call renders training unnecessary. On the other hand, Quakers also can receive a call to specialized ministry, requiring extra training to be faithful to that leading. Trueblood was speaking in particular of pastoral ministry among Quakers. He also was speaking at a time when Quakers were starting an experimental ministry program at Earlham College. The program would later become the denomination's first and only accredited graduate seminary.[1] For Trueblood, the proposed school of ministry would meet the need for equipping those called to specialized ministry among Friends.[2]

If there had been no need for trained pastors in the Religious Society of Friends, founding dean Wil Cooper pointed out, Earlham School of Religion would never have come into being.[3] Since the 19th century, many Western and Midwestern Friends had adopted programmed worship and pastoral leadership. The pastors serving these congregations, however, sometimes had training from other denominations or were so poorly supported or compensated, they left Quaker ministry altogether. As a result, 20th century meetings and churches were losing Quaker identity and vitality, and some Friends developed a concern for Quaker-trained leadership. ESR hoped to

---

[1] As of this writing, Carolina Evangelical Divinity School, a seminary affiliated with the Evangelical Friends church, is a candidate for accreditation with Association of Theological Schools.

[2] Wil Cooper considered Elton Trueblood's articulation of Quaker ministry to be one of the greatest services Trueblood performed for the Religious Society of Friends and for ESR. See D. Elton Trueblood, "The Paradox of the Quaker Ministry," *Quaker Religious Thought* IV, no. 2 (Autumn 1962), 3-15.

[3] Wil Cooper and Tom Mullen, interview by Bill Ratliff, videorecording, 2002.

address that concern by being a school of ministry that would train Friends after the manner of Friends.

What exactly did training for Quaker ministry look like, though? That was the question. Previously there had been a few attempts at training leadership; some programs required one extra year beyond the traditional four-year education at Quaker colleges, and other programs were offered at Bible colleges associated with Friends. These were denominational precedents that did not satisfy Cooper. When he began researching the possibility of a school of ministry in 1959, Cooper had in mind graduate-level education and training specifically for leadership and an approach in education that encouraged students to be persons of "understanding and enlightened judgment."[4]

After traveling around the United States and engaging Friends in conversation, Cooper suggested in the final report that the proposed Quaker seminary give "high priority" to the importance of first-hand religious experience in both the academic and spiritual lives of students, and that such a school should encourage the growth of students as whole persons. He

---

[4]Wil Cooper, *The ESR Story: A Quaker Dream Come True* (Richmond, IN: Earlham School of Religion), 123.

also said neo-orthodox and narrowly fundamentalist theological orientations were not "completely compatible with Quakerism" and encouraged a "Friends approach to the Christian faith." The school should have a "scholarly atmosphere," in which students would study Quakerism and "wrestle with basic problems of religious truth," but there also should be great effort by students and faculty to develop "an intimate Christian fellowship" in the life of the school. Students would ideally "develop a sense of social and political responsibility," but they would also learn practical skills in finance and administration in service to meetings. Cooper acknowledged other types of ministry—teaching, writing, lay, and outreach—but emphasized the current need for pastoral leadership in small, local meetings.[5] During its early years, ESR emphasized the need for pastoral leadership.

Although Cooper was very committed to and interested in training pastoral leadership, he never envisioned that ESR would train *only* pastoral ministers. He shared Elton Trueblood's understanding of ministry based on Spirit-given gifts, which meant the activities constituting ministry were broad

---

[5]Cooper, *ESR Story*, 132-133.

and might even be applied outside the meeting. Ministry was not considered merely speaking during meeting or preaching from the pulpit. This view has challenged and continues to challenge different Friends' understandings of ministry. ESR has maintained during its 50-year history that all people in ministry must be spiritually prepared, centered in prayer, and schooled in Christ. Even in 1959, Cooper hoped ESR would be good ground for cultivating and nurturing the next generation of Friends leadership, whether those Friends were pastors, scholars and teachers, lay workers, or writers.

In Paradox, but Looking Ahead

Many Quakers today are familiar with the tensions underlying the Religious Society of Friends. Some of these tensions are cultural, but others are theological, including, for example, the way Friends think about and practice ministry. Throughout its 50 years, ESR has educated and equipped students for ministry by being true to both a historic understanding of Quaker ministry and to the current perceived needs of the Society.[6] Because Friends have a wide range of understand-

---

[6]Ibid., 27.

ing as to what those ministry needs are and how they should be met, at times ESR has experienced considerable tension with the greater Religious Society of Friends it wishes to serve. By the very nature of its mission to educate and equip for ministry, ESR's existence has been marked and shaped by the struggles and joys of existing both within the tensions of the Religious Society of Friends and within the paradox of Quaker ministry. ESR occupies a middle ground. Here Friends of all persuasions come together to discern and test their sense of calling to ministry. Here in this middle ground of the present, where worship styles, theologies, and spiritualities connect, ESR finds the roots of its past and discerns its vision for the future. Learning to live fruitfully and creatively in the tension has been a lifelong work of the school.

This retrospective focuses primarily on 1985–2010, the second half of ESR's 50 years. During this period, the school has seen physical expansion that included a new building and a partnership with another seminary, which is now located literally next door. Some growth has not been as visual, such as the launch and success of *ESR Access*, an online distance education program that allows students to take courses at ESR without needing to relocate to Richmond. Other growth has been inward and quiet. After careful thought about stewardship and its relationship to donors, ESR decided to opt out of a financial campaign with its parent institution, Earlham College. ESR has renewed its commitment to be in touch with monthly and yearly meetings across the country, and to clarify the school's mission to the larger denomination. ESR also is aware of and living into the intercultural nature of education. Students and professors have traveled to distant countries, both to teach and to learn. The school has also found ways to live creatively in the tension that has so characterized its existence through encouraging different types of Quaker ministry, serving as a resource to the greater Society, and nurturing and releasing the gifts and ministry of non-Quaker students who attend the School of Religion.

In 1960, ESR began as an experiment in Quaker theological education. As the school looks toward its fiftieth anniversary in 2010, ESR celebrates both what it has already accomplished and what it is hoping to accomplish. As a living institution, ESR works to balance continual seeking for direction with confident, steady grounding in the stillness of Christ's presence.

CHAPTER ONE:

THE LIFE AND WORK OF WILMER COOPER AT ESR, 1985

1985 was a typical, and possibly even quiet, year for Earlham School of Religion. Tom Mullen was dean, and students attended classes in the Robert Barclay Center, a building that had once been the home of D. Elton Trueblood, well-known writer, speaker, and former professor. Faculty and students shared the weekly Common Meal in the dining room of this house. Faithful secretary Sue Kern and receptionist Carol Nutter welcomed visitors, typed letters, and answered telephones in Jenkins House, an old building facing National Road. Students lived in the neighboring Lawrence House, and Claudia Ettel, business manager, handled their financial aid. There was something special about what seemed to be an ordinary year for the small Quaker seminary in Richmond, Indiana. ESR was celebrating 25 years of existence, a milestone that some faculty and supporters would not have previously believed possible a few years earlier.

The school, originally begun as an experiment by Earlham College in 1960, was a fully accredited graduate school of ministry, and had been so since 1975. Having struggled to make ends meet for most of its short life, by 1985 ESR was on better financial ground and even had paid the debt owed its parent institution. The school enjoyed strong faculty: Fred Tiffany taught Old Testament; Alan Kolp, New Testament and Early Church History; Hugh Barbour, Church History and Quakerism; Pamela (Peet) Pearson, Applied Theology; Patricia Washburn, Peace and Justice Studies; and John Miller, Theology. ESR graduates were ministering in many different ways— through pastoring and teaching, campus ministry, and writing.

In addition to celebrating ESR's first quarter-century, the school was commemorating another important accomplishment in 1985. Wilmer Cooper, professor of theology and ethics, as well as emeritus founding dean of Earlham School of Religion, was retiring.

Standing on the stage, smiling and surprised, waiting to receive an honorary Doctor of Divinity degree from ESR at the Earlham Commencement, Wil Cooper likely had many things going through his mind. One might have been a memory of himself as a new high school graduate in the late 1930s, sitting over a boiler in his parents' greenhouse in eastern Ohio, feeling a sense of call to important work and service ahead, fully aware he would have to leave his home to do it. No doubt other memories included a 1958 conversation with then-Earlham president Landrum Bolling, who was interested in establishing a Quaker school of ministry on campus and asked Cooper whether he would consider researching the possibility. Cooper agreed and decided to move his wife and young children from Washington, D.C. to Richmond, Indiana. One year, 15,000 miles, and 70 pages later, Cooper handed a feasibility report to Bolling and the Earlham Board of Trustees, and he began work in the fall of 1960 as a religion professor for a fledgling graduate school that utilized Earlham's existing M.A. program in religion. When the Trustees approved the continuation of the School of Religion and a Bachelor of Divinity degree in 1962, they asked Wil Cooper to be dean, a position he held until 1978.

He had worked hard, along with others, to convince Friends to support Earlham School of Religion financially and to help the school gain accreditation from the Association of Theological Schools. He read Quaker periodicals regularly and responded (often in the school's defense) whenever ESR was mentioned. He knew the school needed a good library and hired a consultant to help make that happen. As dean, he kept meticulous notes and numerous folders, keenly aware of the shaping potential of historical events in the life of the school, often saving several copies of important articles. He kept promotional booklets, course catalogs, and newspaper clippings— all items he planned to give to the Friends Collection and Archives at Earlham College's Lilly Library.

Small in stature, but tenacious and persistent, Cooper often voiced his opinion, whether or not it was welcome. He could also be cautious, carefully waiting until he had more information. Feeling strongly about maintaining his and the school's integrity, he even included among his files notes he would have liked to discard, such as the ones he kept when he stepped down as dean. Ever true to character, he attached a note to the notes: *I wondered whether I should throw all of this away.* Realizing that the notes and the struggles they represented were part of ESR's history, he decided not to. He explained that his 1976–77 notes were difficult to understand; they no longer made much sense even to him. Cooper believed in being deliberate and truthful about small details, even if they made him feel personally uncomfortable.

The school was not without its hard times, and Cooper himself was all too aware of this, even as he stood on the stage, waiting to receive the surprise honorary doctorate degree. Once he had been tempted to give up when the 1967 capital campaign seemed to be yielding less than the desired, and necessary, result of $1 million. Former Earlham President Tom Jones scolded Cooper for his lack of faith and vision, and by the end of the calendar year, the money came in and even exceeded the goal. Keeping the school open took effort, and Cooper paid a personal price. Constant worry and stress may have contributed to physical illness, and travel for fundraising often took him away from his wife, Emily, and their four children. In 1978, he stepped down as dean and devoted himself to classroom teaching.

For many years there had been a concern that ESR would be a financial drain on Earlham College, and as recently as 1978–1979, the College assigned a committee to assess

ESR's financial situation, keeping open the possibility of laying the school down as one course of action. After careful consideration, the committee acknowledged ESR's independence and contribution as a seminary, but urged ESR take more responsibility for its finances. Thanks to the leadership and creativity of Dean Alan Kolp and the energy of Board of Trustees member Barbara Perkins, ESR surprised both the College and itself by repaying its debt to Earlham by 1980, much sooner than everyone had anticipated.

Financial concerns aside, ESR reflected a spiritual heritage that was deeply divided. Historically, the Religious Society of Friends was wary of paid leadership and theological education, a position that held steady among Conservative Friends in Cooper's native eastern Ohio, as well as among unprogrammed Friends in the East. Neighboring denominations influenced Friends in the Midwest, who sought education and training for leadership, hoping for a distinctively Quaker education through ESR for their pastors. The irony was, however, that by the late 1970s, the school began to attract unprogrammed Friends, the very ones who had been so critical of the school when it was founded, and these Friends sought grounding in the Bible and in historical Quakerism. Some Conservative

Friends came to the school, as well as a few Evangelical Friends. ESR seemed to be drawing together Friends from different branches of the Quaker family tree.

Perhaps, mused Cooper, still smiling on the Earlham commencement stage, his own life experiences had been his best preparation for founding and helping to run a school that, through no effort of his, attracted Quakers at different places on the theological spectrum. Before he even got to Richmond, Indiana, Cooper had experience with three different kinds of Friends. His upbringing in eastern Ohio was unprogrammed and deeply Christ-centered, and he worshipped with programmed Friends during his undergraduate years at Wilmington College. Cooper also worked for the Friends Council on National Legislation, an organization run by mostly unprogrammed Friends. The school for which he worked so hard had begun to serve all three of these groups.

On that bright, sunny day in June of 1985, Wil Cooper brought his thoughts back to the present and finished listening to Tom Mullen read a citation that granted him an honorary doctorate degree for his service to Earlham School of Religion, a school that had played a central role in his calling and life's work. Cooper already had four other academic degrees, and one of them was a doctorate. It was, however, for this degree that he probably had worked the longest and the hardest.

As Cooper walked out of the graduation ceremony with the degree in hand, he felt a sense of accomplishment, but he also was aware of much more that needed to be done. ESR had long outgrown its current set of buildings. The Robert Barclay Center was now a tight fit. Students and faculty crammed into the hallway to talk and wait while the Common Meal was being prepared in the kitchen. The dining room was also a classroom. Rooms served multiple functions, and the afternoon class couldn't begin until the dishes were cleared and washed. Across the way, Jenkins House had leaks. ESR really needed a new building, and RBC needed major remodeling. Something had to be done soon.

But for now, Cooper was going to celebrate. He would go to the banquet honoring him and Emily, and he would find it attended by more than 300 people. There would also be a four-layer cake. He would see and talk to alumni/ae, and attend workshops led by former faculty members. He would also learn of a very important gift: the Wil and Emily Cooper Scholarship fund for future ESR students. Cooper, of course, had no intention of leaving the school after his retirement. He would continue to teach courses in Quakerism and even write *A Living Faith: an Historical and Comparative Study of Friends Beliefs.* But first he would celebrate, because it was time.

CHAPTER TWO:

GROWING YEARS: 1985–1990

A New Building

When Wil Cooper retired in 1985, plans already were underway for a new building at ESR. Space had been tight in Robert Barclay Center for years, but the school had not been in a position to consider seriously the financial aspect of expanding the facilities. With the debt to Earlham College paid off, ESR turned to planning for a new building and raising the funds to pay for it.

As early as 1983, ESR's Board of Advisors began considering where the new building might be located. One possibility was to build "adjacent to the west side of Stout Meetinghouse," which would put ESR in close proximity to Carpenter Hall and Lilly Library. Another possibility was to remain at the corner of National Road and College Avenue. The Advisors eventually chose to stay at the current site, perhaps to keep ESR's "image and identity" as a graduate theological school separate from the College's.[7]

The following year the Board of Advisors formed an Expansion Committee to make plans for "improving ESR's facilities."[8] This committee considered the school's needs and priorities for the new building. ESR needed space for classrooms, but it also needed space for community life and activities, such as worship and Common Meal. In the spring of 1986, the Expansion Committee estimated the cost of the project at approximately $2 million, which included the new building itself, furnishings and maintenance, and renovations for the existing Robert Barclay Center.[9] By the fall, the ESR Development

---

[7]ESR, Board of Advisors Annual Meeting Minutes, November 12-14, 1983, 4.

[8]ESR, Board of Advisors Annual Meeting Minutes, November 11-12, 1984, 8.

[9]ESR, Board of Advisors Executive Board Minutes, March 14, 1986, 2.

Committee had researched and planned for a major capital campaign to raise funds for the building and renovations.

The Expansion Committee chose the Pescok, Jelliffe, Randall, and Nice architectural firm from Indianapolis to design and construct the new building at ESR's location. Representatives from the firm visited ESR and spent time talking with students and faculty, as well as observing the flow of community life. Noticing how students crowded into RBC before Common Meal as well as the importance of communal interaction, the architect designed a large gathering area in the direct path to all other parts of the building, including the dining room, a large kitchen with an industrial-size dishwasher, and the worship room, which was set back from National Road and College Avenue as far as possible to minimize noise from outside traffic. Small rooms for study and meditation were located down a hallway on the first floor for privacy. Classrooms were built on the second floor, which could be accessed by stairs. Earlier ideas for the new building included a fireplace, but since it was not the most cost-effective option, ESR chose instead to add an elevator and a small circular window on a second floor interior wall overlooking the gathering area.

In addition to taking ESR's community life and educational purpose into account for the building's interiors, the architectural firm considered Quaker identity when designing
the exterior, which was gray fieldstone. This puzzled College
faculty and other community members because it did not
match the other red brick buildings on campus. The stone,
however, gave the ESR building an aged look resembling
meetinghouses found in the Delaware Valley,[10] a region associated with the foundations of American Quakerism. Other aspects of the building also reflected the school's Quaker identity,
such as the porch typical of some meetinghouses in the East,
and numerous windows to let in light, perhaps as a theological
statement.[11] Drawing on historic American meeting house architecture in the East gave ESR a sense of establishment and
participation in Friends tradition. Yet the building also took
into account its more immediate surroundings; some people
looked at the architectural sketch of the new building and noticed a resemblance to Stout Meetinghouse on the College

---

[10]Thomas D. Hamm, *Earlham College: A History* (Bloomington, IN: Indiana University Press, 1997), 336.

[11]"Purpose Dictates Form of New ESR Building," *ESR Reports* (Spring
1987), 1.

campus.[12] In this way, the school carries influence from different regions of American Quakerism in its very architecture.

Work began in spring 1988 with the demolition of Jenkins House. Staff offices were moved to RBC, where they continue to this day, and classes and worship were held in Jones House on the College campus while the new building was under construction. By mid-summer, workers were laying and pouring the foundation, and by early fall, they had installed steel undergirding and first floor beams.[13] By the time the building was completed and ready for occupancy in September 1989, ESR spent a little over $2 million, with $1.5 million on the building; $500,000 on furnishings, equipment, and landscaping; and $300,000 on Robert Barclay Center renovations.[14] When the 1989–1990 school year began, faculty and students were pleased with the new building, and so, apparently, was everyone else. One of the biggest challenges that fall involved

---

[12]Ibid.

[13]Scott Hinkley, "New Building Update," *Nexus* (Fall 1988), 7.

[14]"New ESR building ready for occupancy," *Earlhamite* 109 (Fall 1989), 3.

working with outside groups who wanted to use the building to hold events.[15]

Tom Mullen and Keith Esch

The new building would not have become a reality without Tom Mullen and Keith Esch's hard work in fundraising during 1985–1990. The *Making a Difference* campaign brought in $5.3 million, considerably more than the original $4.5 million goal. Outside consultants doubted that ESR would reach $4.5 million, and many guessed $2.5 million was a more reasonable estimate. "We're delighted the experts were wrong," Mullen wrote. He and Esch traveled on the weekends, campaigning in all parts of the country, going as far west as California and as far east as Philadelphia.[16] They made sure that they returned in time for classes on Tuesday morning because Mullen, in addition to his duties as dean, also taught courses.

Mullen was a man with many gifts and abilities. He served as Dean of Students at Earlham College, taught Applied

---

[15]John Miller, "Report of the Academic Dean to the ESR Board of Advisors," October 26, 1989.

[16]Tom Mullen, "The Dream and the Dreamers," *ESR Reports* (November/December 1990), 1-2.

Studies at ESR since the 1970s, and became Dean of Earlham School of Religion in 1984 after Alan Kolp returned to teaching. Unlike both his predecessors, Mullen did not hold a doctorate, although he came with experience in administration at Earlham College and pastoral work in Indiana Yearly Meeting. He had also served as Acting Dean a few times for Alan Kolp and Wil Cooper. Mullen's humor, kind nature, and skills in public speaking served him well on the campaign trail. Thanks to his reputation as a popular speaker and writer, he enjoyed Friends' approval and support across the theological spectrum.[17] Mullen continued teaching after his retirement in 1990, sometimes leading courses related to pastoral ministry, but devoting much of his time to creating and teaching the Ministry of Writing program.

Mullen relied heavily on the organizational skills of Keith Esch, a 1966 ESR graduate, who joined the staff in 1969. Esch came to ESR in 1964 with a Mennonite background and an interest in the ways Friends did pastoral ministry, specifically the concept and practice of team ministry. He served the Mennonite church before transferring his membership to

---

[17]John Miller, interview with author, 2-12-2009.

Friends some years later. Esch considered work at ESR his vocation. Until his retirement from ESR in 1993, he most often filled roles related to recruitment, development, and business management, all things central to ESR's viability as an institution. Esch's ability to organize enabled the success of different programs at ESR. In addition to research for the 1985 campaign, he organized travel and locations for the Valiant Sixty[18] recruitment method Alan Kolp developed during his deanship. Esch's development experience also made him nearly impossible to replace after he retired. "No one knew nation-wide gifts and prospects like Keith Esch," said Katharine Jacobsen, who was also on ESR's development staff.[19] Like Wil Cooper and Tom Mullen, Esch continued his involvement with the school after retirement. He served on the Earlham Board of Trustees for nine years and also was liaison to the ESR Board of Advisors.

---

[18]*Valiant Sixty* refers to the number of men George Fox sent out to preach and spread word of the Friends message in the 1600s. ESR did not aspire to duplicate that effort, but the school did intend to visit schools and meetings in the "spirit of reaching out in ministry," much like early Friends. A school-wide effort, faculty and students participated in this very successful outreach and recruitment method. See "ESR's Valiant Sixty," *ESR Reports* (Spring 1972), 2.

[19]Katharine Jacobsen, interview with author, 2-27-2009.

Sense of Community

In the late 1950s, Wil Cooper envisioned ESR as a place where students and faculty might develop an intimate Christian fellowship. A weekly practice from the early days of the school, Common Meal was—and continues to be—one way ESR embodies this vision. Every week, students and faculty gathered for food, fellowship, and a program. For many years, the programs tended to be lecture-discussions, but today, programs range in variety from lighthearted games to more serious presentations by faculty, students, or outside speakers. Faculty, staff, and students help to clean up and wash the dishes. Common Meal is a time when the entire school can have fun, learn, and even mourn together. One student recalled a Common Meal in 1986 when Tom Mullen announced that the space shuttle Challenger had exploded: "It was a startling announcement and I needed a pastor. Tom guided us skillfully though a time of reflection and prayer." After Common Meal moved to the dining room of the new building, ESR students, faculty, staff, and visitors held hands and formed a circle in the new gathering area, had a brief time of sharing, and then held the joys and concerns of the community in prayer before eating.

For three decades, ESR held a monthly meeting for business that was open to the entire school community. The monthly meeting allowed faculty and staff to make decisions together, but it also revealed some difficulties inherent in ESR's identity. Although ESR is a Quaker, spiritual community, ESR is also an institution, not its own meeting-congregation. Corporate discernment and decision-making are difficult to practice in an institution because built-in structures automatically give some persons more authority than others, and some matters are not open for corporate input. The Friends principles that guide spiritual, congregational life are not always easily transferable to institutional life, and this is a challenging aspect of ESR's identity. By the early 1990s, faculty and students formed separate meetings to consider different items of business, but the practice of listening carefully and seeking Divine guidance in each meeting continues. In recent years, there has been more faculty-student interaction in community business. Student clerks have regularly attended faculty meetings, presented student concerns, and reported back to the students. Students often send observers to meetings held by the Board of Trustees and Board of Advisors. Faculty also will sometimes invite students to join specific school committees, when appropriate.[20]

At all times in ESR's history, the school held worship regularly. In the 1980s, worship occurred every day that classes were scheduled and alternated between programmed and unprogrammed styles.[21] With Bethany's arrival in the mid-90s came a weekly joint-seminary worship service, as well as monthly joint Common Meals. Less formal times for fellowship also developed among students and faculty at the school. Students often went to gatherings in each other's homes, and faculty visited with each other outside the workplace. It was also quite common for students to walk into Jenkins House or Robert Barclay Center and chat with receptionist Phyllis Wetherell, who was known as "the face of ESR" during her 15-year tenure at the school. Much of this informal fellowship still occurs at ESR, although several current and former faculty say they miss "the good old days" when they sensed a deeper and closer community connection.

Although the present-day ESR community is more loosely structured than some faculty, students, and alumni/ae

---

[20]*Self-Study Report for the Association of Theological Schools* (2006), 16.

would like, the people who now comprise the community come with different experiences and priorities. Student life stages range from recent college graduates to grandparents, a marked difference from the very early days of ESR, when most students came directly from their undergraduate experiences. During the 1980s and 1990s, students tended to be older, often in their 30s. Some current students are commuters and are on campus only on a weekly basis; others are part-time due to economic necessity; others are parents supporting families. For these students, spending time with the community may not happen at the more obvious places, such as the gathering area sofas or around a table at Common Meal. The classroom itself becomes the place where community happens, and *ESR Access* offers a sense of online community for those who learn away from campus. In order to facilitate this kind of interaction, the faculty continues to take care to cultivate a classroom atmosphere that encourages listening, sharing, and prayer.

---

[21]Cooper, *ESR Story*, 86.

Women at ESR

Women in the Religious Society of Friends have participated in ministry and business since the 1600s in England. Some women undertook dangerous journeys and endured public ridicule as they preached, and others died at the hands of the Puritans in colonial America, including Mary Dyer, whose statue stands outside Earlham College's Stout Meetinghouse. Given this denominational history, it is interesting that women were clearly in the minority for most of ESR's first 25 years. Women were welcome to attend the school, and they did—ESR's first graduating class in 1963 had three students, and one was a woman—but during the 1960s and 1970s, women attending seminary was simply not a cultural norm. In fact, a very early ESR application form assumed the applicant was male; one of the questions asked whether or not the applicant's wife would be working while he was taking classes. The question was probably designed to assess the (male) student's financial situation. Even though ESR followed American cultural trends in assuming most applicants were male, the school's distinctive Quaker atmosphere was already present. Wives and families were welcome—and even encouraged—to take part in ESR community and intellectual life, as were husbands and fiancés.[22]

In 1976, Tom Mullen noticed the number of enrolled women students at ESR had almost doubled in a matter of five years. He pointed out that this was a trend in other seminaries as well.[23] The number of enrolled women exceeded that of the men for the first time in the 1980–1981 school year.[24] The number of women in ESR's graduating classes also slowly increased. In 1986, the numbers of men and women in the graduating class had reached 50 percent, and for nearly the rest of the decade, there were often more women graduating than men, a continuing tendency, for the most part, to the present day. Wil Cooper later said he never expected so many women to come to the school.[25] Cultural expectations in American society have changed over the decades, and the balance of women and men in ESR's graduating classes reflect this cultural tendency.

---

[22]ESR *Catalog* (1964-66), 19.

[23]Tom Mullen, "Truth in Statistics," *Earlhamite* 97 (Winter 1976), 12.

[24]Cooper, *ESR Story*, Appendix IV (a).

[25]Wil Cooper and Tom Mullen, interview.

As the numbers of men and women in ESR's graduating classes equalized in the mid-1980s, the school also sought to appoint more women to its faculty. Miriam Burke, Associate Professor of Counseling and Pastoral Psychology from 1972–1983, was at that point in time ESR's longest, full-time female faculty member. For much of her ESR career, she was the only one. Pamela (Peet) Pearson joined the faculty as Assistant Professor of Applied Theology in 1982, followed by Patricia Washburn as Assistant Professor Peace and Justice Studies in 1985. In 1987, ESR appointed Judith Middleton Applegate, a 1982 ESR graduate, as Assistant Professor of New Testament Studies, and in 1989, Ann Miller, a 1985 graduate, came as Director of Field Education. Nancy Bowen, Associate Professor of Old Testament, joined the faculty in 1991, and she is currently one of the more senior faculty members. As ESR's 50th year approaches, the ESR regular teaching faculty is nearing 50 percent, with five men and four women.

The equalized and increased numbers of women at ESR during the 1980s corresponded to a greater cultural awareness of feminism and women's issues. Unlike other seminaries whose denominations had prohibited women from leadership, ESR did not have to work against long-held denominational

views keeping women from leadership positions and ordina-
tion.[26] The school did, however, engage larger cultural and his-
torical issues relating to women, the church, and images of
God. Many students read theologians and scholars such as
Elizabeth Schüssler-Fiorenza, Sallie McFague, and Phyllis
Trible.

ESR adopted an inclusive language statement in 1986.
Believing the human unity found in Christ as stated in Gala-
tians 3:28, the ESR community committed to using "inclusive
language in all our worship, speaking, and writing." Human
unity could be broken through "exclusive use of male language
for God" and using "black/white imagery to describe an
evil/good situation."[27] The inclusive language statement was
challenging for some students at first, and occasionally a student still struggles with it. ESR faculty members usually go
over the statement with incoming classes. For the most part,
though, inclusive language is woven into the community fabric

---

[26]Although the Religious Society of Friends does have a testimony of
equality, the denomination has not been immune to gender discrimination
and bias in ministry.

[27]"Inclusive Language Statement," ESR *Catalog* (2004–2007), 10.

and has simply become part of the school's everyday life and practice.

Making Room: Hospitality and Community

Many students appreciate ESR for its hospitable atmosphere. Former faculty members described the school in its "good old days" as family-like, perhaps because classes and Common Meal took place in a former residence. The small, tight space encouraged closeness, and students worried the new ESR building's larger size would erode community life. Because some describe present community life as "looser" than it once was, maybe the new building did play a role in changing the way people interacted. At the same time, changes in student population and economic situations also contributed to this change. Yet ESR consistently makes room, both literally and figuratively. The new ESR building has large worship, dining, and gathering spaces. It even has a commuter lounge equipped with a sofa and a shower. Students and faculty seek to be hospitable to each other's different understandings and experiences of God, and when latecomers slip into the pre-Common Meal time of prayer and sharing, no one thinks twice about reaching for the newcomer's hands. The community circle simply opens and adjusts, making the circle even bigger.

CHAPTER THREE:

STRETCHING YEARS: THE EARLY 1990S

Disappointment in ESR

The early 1990s were not easy times for ESR. The school had entered its fourth decade, and ESR was experiencing growing pains. Unprogrammed Friends' initial doubt and skepticism in the 1960s about the school had faded and now gave way to disappointment and dissatisfaction, particularly within Indiana Yearly Meeting. ESR had been founded and funded with the purpose of preparing pastoral leadership for Friends, and it appeared to some that ESR was failing to fulfill its original purpose.

Disappointment in the school had roots in trends starting at least a decade earlier. In the late 1970s, a number of unprogrammed Friends from the East began attending ESR, much
to both Wil Cooper and Tom Mullen's surprise.[28] Mullen was
pleased with the theological diversity these students brought
to the school; Cooper noticed the change in student population
and commented, "This is one of the longterm [sic] trends which
needs to be assessed carefully."[29] There was also a "shift in
student interests" at ESR in the 1980s, perhaps related to the
population changes, which now drew a greater number of students from yearly meetings affiliated with Friends General
Conference. Although training for pastoral ministry continued
to draw students from Friends United Meeting, more students
were coming to the school with different career goals in ministry, such as chaplaincy, counseling, and administration.[30]
Through some unanticipated shifts in student population and
interests, ESR was going in a direction that not all Friends ap-

---

[28]Wil Cooper and Tom Mullen, interview.

[29]Tom Mullen, interview with author, 10-27-2008; Cooper, *ESR Story*,
64.

[30]Hamm, *Earlham College: a History*, 335.

preciated; the school seemed to be less interested in preparing pastoral ministers.

Another factor may also have contributed to declining student interest in pastoral ministry at ESR. Membership within the Religious Society of Friends in North America has been in steady decline since the 1970s. Membership in Friends United Meeting in particular saw a significant decrease between 1962 and 1992. Although statistics can be read and understood in a number of ways, the declining numbers suggest there were fewer Friends affiliated with Friends United Meeting, the body of Friends that Earlham School of Religion had originally meant to serve. In 1962, two years after ESR's founding, the total number of Friends affiliated with Friends United Meeting was 52,101; in 1992, that number had dropped to 32,520. The number of Friends jointly affiliated with Friends United Meeting and Friends General Conference decreased slightly from 17,029 in 1972 to 14,150 in 1992.[31]

---

[31]Marty Sulek, *Case for Support* (2005), B–12.

ESR's Liberal Image

Some Friends in Indiana Yearly Meeting were concerned about ESR faculty and the nature of the instruction students were receiving. Believing the faculty had "limited pastoral experience" and the perspective from which Bible courses
were taught was "insufficiently evangelical," the yearly meeting's executive committee in 1991 approved a proposal to es-
tablish an alternative plan of study for Quaker ministry at
Anderson School of Theology, which is affiliated with the
Church of God. Three students later chose the "Anderson Alternative."[32] While the alternative did not attract many students who would have ordinarily gone to ESR, the situation
was nevertheless problematic for ESR's reputation. "We are
feeling the effects of the 'Anderson Alternative,'" Keith Esch
wrote in the 1992 Recruitment Planning Report. "ESR's liberal
image is a problem for many, especially those considering pastoral ministry."[33]

---

[32]Hamm, *Earlham College: a History*, 341; Indiana Yearly Meeting Executive Committee Minutes, 1991, Friends Collection and Archives.

[33]"Recruitment Planning Report: Earlham School of Religion," Earlham
Board of Trustees Minutes, February 17, 1992, 74.

Yet it was not simply the school's liberal image that concerned the yearly meeting; it was also ESR faculty who seemed to be engaging in non-Christian practices. In the fall of 1990, rumors of witchcraft and other pagan rituals taking place at ESR circulated among Indiana Friends. These rumors started when Friends outside the school learned a professor had listed *Motherpeace Tarot Cards* as one of seven supplemental texts on the syllabus for a feminist spirituality course. Using or reading the cards, however, was not a requirement for the class; not even real tarot cards, they were intended as supplemental material to help students understand the work and thought of secular feminists. In response to concerned Friends and supporters of ESR, faculty approved and distributed a minute affirming the school's Christian Quaker commitment. This minute did not satisfy all Indiana Friends. In 1991, the yearly meeting clerk continued to see Anderson School of Theology as a "more Christian" alternative to getting a Quaker seminary education.[34]

---

[34]Hamm, *Earlham College: a History*, 341-42; John Miller correspondence, December 12, 1990 and ESR Faculty Minute, November 26, 1990, papers from the Office of the President; John Miller interview, 2-12-2009; Stacy Kawamura, "IYM Proposes to Support Anderson Quaker Professor," *Earlham Word*, October 25, 1991.

Tensions

The early 1990s were difficult for ESR, but the years were also a time of sharp tension within the greater Religious Society of Friends, particularly Friends United Meeting. FUM was considering realignment among meetings along particular theological understandings of Jesus Christ and "the role of the Bible as a source of religious authority."[35] The proposal caused a great deal of pain within FUM, especially for Friends who identified as liberal. Although the proposal did not have "widespread support," it nevertheless reflected a growing frustration among more evangelically leaning Friends who wanted a clear position to unify FUM and make it a more effective organization.[36] Friends not in favor of the realignment proposal saw it as divisive.

While ESR was not involved in FUM's realignment proposal, the school experienced similar tension between evangelical and liberal theological understandings of Christianity and Quakerism. Some students who identified as evangelicals

---

[35]Stephen Main, "Realignment: When Core Values Collide," in *Realignment: Nine Views Among Friends* (Wallingford, PA: Pendle Hill, Monday Evening Lecture Series, Autumn 1991), 14–16.

[36]Bill Samuel, "Realignment Among North American Friends?" Available at: http://www.quakerinfo.com/quakalig.shtml (accessed 2-17-2009).

felt alienated at ESR and saw the faculty—even the school—as hostile to evangelical points of view. For other students who were in the process of preparing for pastoral ministry, ESR's liberal position on feminism—in particular, the inclusive language statement—did not fit well with the positions of some meetings or churches where students were already pastoring. Some students also wished ESR would offer a more evangelical articulation of its Christian spiritual foundations.[37] In the midst of these concerns, Keith Esch noticed that ESR was also trying to "serve unprogrammed Friends," and the "most liberal" Quaker students considered the school "too conservative theologically and much too 'churchy.'" ESR found itself in the middle of a much larger cultural and denominational tension. "We need to continue to challenge both camps," wrote Esch, "and to create with self-confidence our own tenable Christian and Quaker ground."[38]

---

[37]"Meeting with ESR Student/Pastors," ESR Board of Advisors Executive Committee Minutes, May 10, 1991, 57–60.

[38]"Recruitment Planning Report," Earlham Board of Trustees Minutes, February 17, 1992, 74.

Changing Times

After Tom Mullen retired in 1990, he left Earlham School of Religion with a new building and a successful financial campaign. He took a brief sabbatical, and then he continued teaching courses at ESR in his retirement. Mullen maintained a campus presence for a number of years. Professor John Miller agreed to serve as interim dean until someone else was hired to fill the position. For the first time in ESR's history, it was not clear who the school's next dean was to be. Wil Cooper, Alan Kolp, and Tom Mullen had been teachers before they served as deans, and no current ESR professors stepped forward to take on the position. A national search yielded eight candidates, and when the interviews were over, Andrew Grannell, a Friend from New England Yearly Meeting, became ESR's fourth dean in 1991.

Although he did not have connections to the school through teaching, Grannell was no stranger to Earlham College or to the School of Religion. He graduated from Earlham in 1965 and earned a Master of Ministry degree from ESR in 1969. In the mid-1980s he chaired a committee that developed a joint Peace Studies program for two schools in Minnesota—St. John's University and the College of St. Benedict—an experience that later proved useful during his ESR career. Grannell was excited for ESR in the "coming decade," which he hoped would be a more "self-confident and generative phase" for the school.[39]

ESR as a Friends Center for the Revitalization of Ministry

As ESR was in the process of discerning and entering into partnership with Bethany Theological Seminary, the school continued to struggle with understanding its identity, role, and purpose. Old ways of being and doing were not working well anymore. Friends inside and outside the school felt ESR had become too insular with no sense of what the rest of the Society needed. The concern was legitimate, and the school was in a difficult place trying to figure out what those needs were, especially since ESR tried to serve students on both sides of the theological divide. Student interests had changed, but so had the very cultural landscape in which ESR operated. Half of ESR's student population was women, and there were more unprogrammed than programmed Friends attending, despite

---

[39]"An Installation Celebration at ESR" program bulletin, November 2, 1991, Wilmer Cooper Papers, Friends Collection and Archives, Richmond, IN.

past recruitment efforts to keep the numbers balanced. The changing atmosphere was not just inside ESR; Friends United Meeting was facing its own questions about its identity and purpose because of decreasing membership. Friends wanted renewal, and FUM sought it through realignment. ESR also sought it through a realignment, but a different kind.

Shortly after Andy Grannell became ESR's new dean, he attended the 1991 Indiana Yearly Meeting sessions. There he expressed hope for revitalization in the Religious Society of Friends and reported that many Friends he met in his travels saw ESR as a "very significant center." Grannell's vision for the school was a "Friends center for the revitalization of ministry," an idea he later wrote about in the fall of the same year. Grannell believed ESR needed to see itself in and part of the larger Religious Society of Friends by claiming Quaker denominational history and learning from it. He also wanted the school to be present to the "ethical and moral dilemmas of our time." Grannell called for a return to the original "springs from which Friends ministry flowed" by "attending to the promptings of our hearts" in a hurting world.[40] He was, in effect, calling for a return to urgent, deeply felt Spirit-led ministry.

Grannell's call was already being answered in part. For quite some time, ESR faculty members had been developing the school's Quaker distinctiveness by adding courses or faculty appointments in spirituality, peace and justice studies, and Quaker studies. Such courses and appointments were not meant only to be intellectual exercises; ESR's aim was to educate whole persons. For student Ken Jacobsen, the classroom was an occasion to have a "meeting for worship for learning," not a forum for mere intellectual discussion.[41] Courses in spirituality, peace and justice, and Quakerism were designed to equip and prepare students for life-giving, empowering Friends ministry.

Preparation for Ministry through Discernment

The school's commitment to and practice of Quakerism created a culture of discernment through constant attention to God's activity in individual lives and in community life as a

---

[40] Andrew P. Grannell, "On Becoming a Friends Center for the Revitalization of Ministry," *ESR Reports* (Fall 1991): 1–2.

[41] Ken Jacobsen, interview with author, 2-27-2009.

whole. Using discernment as a means "to be with God and each other" is a distinguishing feature of the school.[42] During Alan Kolp's deanship, the faculty seriously considered the way in which Quakers practice spirituality and considered how it might be better integrated into the curriculum. Out of that process, Miriam Burke developed a course called Spiritual Preparation for Ministry, which helps students attend to their personal spiritual journeys through journaling, spiritual friendships, and other spiritual disciplines. It has been required for first-semester Master of Divinity/Ministry students since the late 1980s.[43] Field Education director Ann Miller was also instrumental in bringing discernment practice to the curriculum, especially when it came to helping students better sense their calls to ministry.

Before the early 1990s, students met individually with professors to talk about areas of giftedness and strength or weakness, and the faculty looked into possibilities for a student's field experience based on that set of conversations. In 1993, Miller changed this procedure in a major way by creating

---

[42]Jay Marshall, interview with author, 10-29-2008.

[43]*Earlham School of Religion Self-Study Report for the Association of Theological Schools* (2006), 34.

a course called the Discernment and Call of Gifts for Ministry. The new course allowed students to identify and discern leadings in a formal way, as well as to receive academic credit for having participated in the process. Students become aware of their gifts in a variety of ways. Through readings and class exercises, students made a profile of their gifts in ministry, which included personality type, previous work or ministry experiences, natural abilities and acquired skills, and spiritual gifts. At the end of the course, students assembled clearness committees in which they tested their sense of call to ministry in a community setting. The committees provided confirmation or guidance for the students. Based on the gifts profile, sense of call, and the clearness committee experience, students better articulated their present call to ministry. Out of this semester-long process, students considered options for a field education placement that corresponded to their call and gifts.

The new discernment course also helped students to declare a particular ministry emphasis, which became a requirement after 1992 for students in the Master of Divinity/Ministry program. Ann Miller, a 1985 ESR graduate, had spent an entire school year doing ministry among unprogrammed Friends in Philadelphia Yearly Meeting as part of her field education. Grateful for a ministry "setting that corresponded" to her "particular call to ministry," Miller wanted to offer such an experience to ESR students.[44] After a review of the Field Education program in 1992, the faculty developed a set of emphases or concentrations to allow students to focus on a particular area of interest. Declaring ministry emphases gave students more guidance in choosing courses that would help them develop necessary skills for their careers in ministry. With Miller's new course in discernment, students were then better able distinguish a ministry emphasis, which could be pastoral ministry, pastoral care and counseling, teaching, peace and justice, Christian spirituality, writing, or ministry among unprogrammed Friends.

Ministry through Peace and Justice Studies

One of Wil Cooper's stated goals for a proposed Friends school of ministry in 1959 was for students to develop a sense of social and political responsibility. He based this goal on Friends' historic peace testimony, as well as the justice and advocacy work done by many Friends over the past few hundred

---

[44]Ann Miller, interview with author, 1-29-2009.

years. Justice and advocacy in Quaker history was something Andrew Grannell especially hoped ESR would continue to claim and strengthen.

Faculty worked to develop this Quaker distinctive. For some years, Wil Cooper coordinated the Peace and Justice Studies program. Patricia Washburn taught peace and justice courses after Wil Cooper's retirement, and Lonnie Valentine, 1983 ESR graduate, joined the faculty in Peace and Justice Studies after Washburn left in 1989. Valentine, a strong believer in teaching peace and justice through all the theological disciplines, developed The Bible and Violence and Nonviolence, History of Friends' Peace Witness, and The Spirituality of Peacemaking, in addition to teaching courses in theology. Valentine also teaches conflict resolution and directs M.A. students whose theses focus on peace and justice issues.

When Bethany Theological Seminary moved next door to ESR in 1994, Valentine and then-Bethany professor Jeffrey Bach created Peace Forum, a weekly event sponsored by the Peace departments at both seminaries. Peace Forum, held in the ESR dining room, offers lunch and features one or more speakers giving presentations on peace-related topics. The Forum is open to the public, and Earlham College students and

Richmond community members often attend. Today, Valentine, Bethany professor Scott Holland, and students from both seminaries oversee the planning and operation of Peace Forum. Through worship, food, fellowship, and presentations, ESR and Bethany offer the seminary and larger communities information and opportunities for action on what Grannell called the "ethical and moral dilemmas of our time."

Ministry Through Quaker Studies

Learning Friends history was also an important aspect of Grannell's vision for ESR. The school had already benefited from the contributions of Hugh Barbour, Wil Cooper, Alan Kolp, and John Miller. ESR sought a full-time appointment in Quaker Studies when Cooper finished teaching in his retirement. In 1991, John Punshon joined the faculty as Geraldine C. Leatherock Professor of Quaker Studies. As author of *Portrait in Grey: A Short History of the Quakers* and several other publications, Punshon brought considerable experience in Quaker life and history.

Punshon's perspective as a British Friend placed him inside the Friends tradition but somewhat outside the American one. Although he had studied the Gurneyite tradition, he looked forward to learning "to know pastoral Quakerism from the inside."[45] Committed to offering courses in both Evangelical and Liberal Quakerism, Punshon hoped "the liberals will do Evangelical Quakerism and evangelicals Liberalism, in the interest of greater Friendly co-operation and understanding."[46] He also conducted several "Quaker Tours" in England for trustees and supporters of ESR. These tours included visits to several places important to early Quakerism, including Firbank Fell and Pendle Hill, as well as Swarthmoor Hall.[47] During a time of great tension in American Quakerism, Punshon offered ESR students, faculty, and community a sense of balance as well as earnest hope for the future of the Religious Society of Friends.

ESR's Sense of Identity and Mission

Besides adding ministry emphases and further developing Quaker distinctives, ESR faculty and students spent time

---

[45]John Punshon, "The Work Ahead: Thoughts and Hopes," *ESR Reports* (Fall 1991), 3.

[46]Punshon, "Quaker Studies at ESR," *ESR Reports* (Spring 1992), 3.

[47]Punshon, e-mail message to the author, 5-15-2009; "Visit the Birthplace of Quakerism," n.p., n.d.

considering the school's role and purpose by revisiting ESR's mission statement. A statement from the mid-1980s focused more on what ESR wanted to *be* and less on what the school was trying to *do*. The 1986 statement read:

> Earlham School of Religion strives to be a seeking, caring seminary community in the tradition of Friends. It attempts to nurture "the examined life" in terms of the Quaker testimonies of integrity, simplicity, equality, community, and non-violence. ESR's main purpose is to prepare men and women for ministry, and it tries to attract persons who are spiritually vital and intentional in their sense of calling.[48]

ESR recognized its purpose to prepare men and women for ministry, but *being* a nurturing, caring Friends community was a worthy goal that sometimes got in the way of ministry preparation. To some Friends inside and outside the school, ESR students and faculty were too preoccupied with being a nurturing place for emotionally hurting people than to be concerned with ministry in a multicultural world—or even being in contact with other Friends. The isolation may have been a defense mechanism. ESR, after all, spent much of its first quarter-century defending its existence, and the school had recently been under severe criticism from other Friends bodies. Despite

---

[48]*Earlham School of Religion ATS Accreditation Self-Study* (1986), 4.

this pain, however, ESR needed to grow and become sure of its role. In 1995, the school decided to "focus" its mission statement because ESR had just entered partnership with Bethany. ESR faculty, students, the Board of Advisors, and the Board of Trustees discerned this sense of mission:

> The mission of the Earlham School of Religion as a Quaker theological school grows out of our belief that God calls every Christian to ministry. Earlham School of Religion prepares women and men of all branches of Friends, and other traditions and faiths, for leadership that empowers and equips the ministry of others. The School encourages students to explore the intellectual, spiritual, and practical dimensions to their calls to ministry.[49]

The 1995 mission statement focused more specifically on what ESR wanted to *do*, that is, to prepare women and men for leadership and ministry, what the preparation entailed, and what such preparation meant to the school. Educating the whole person, an ESR goal since 1960, remained in the mission statement, as did the school's Quaker identity. *Being* a Friends school of religion still mattered deeply to ESR, but now it was time to focus on being more *outwardly directed* in that identity. Mentioning non-Quakers in the statement named the ecumeni-

---

[49] *Self-Study Report for Accreditation Review* (1996), 5.

cal quality of ESR's present atmosphere, and the mission statement also used the word *equip*, a word that had been in the school's vocabulary since 1960. The re-focused mission statement was a step forward for ESR to gain a better sense of its purpose as a Friends school of ministry, and also as an educational and ecumenical partner with Bethany Theological Seminary.

The beginning of the decade saw Friends United Meeting, and specifically Indiana Yearly Meeting, disappointed with ESR because the school was not producing as many pastors as the yearly meeting would have liked. There was also great tension between Friends in the United States about particular theological understandings and cultural practices. As a Friends body, ESR reflected the greater tension because some students who went to ESR were theologically divided. In an effort to revitalize the wider Religious Society of Friends through ESR, Grannell urged the School to reclaim Friends' authentic, Spirit-led ministry. The school continued developing its Quaker distinctiveness by building on important aspects in the Friends tradition, such as aiding students to discern their calls to ministry, providing solid theological grounding and training for peace and justice work, and by enabling ESR to gain a better understanding of Friends life and history with a full-time professor in Quaker Studies.

ESR's culture of discernment helped the school in many ways. Besides giving students a course through which to better understand their call and gifts and the means to name a ministry emphasis, discernment and review enabled ESR corporately to re-focus its sense of mission in 1995. As the school became more focused on outwardly directing its sense of identity, ministry emphases and particular Quaker distinctives became natural, spiritual outpourings. In other words, ESR lived into itself and became *more* Quaker in the process.

CHAPTER FOUR:

BETHANY THEOLOGICAL SEMINARY

When new Dean Andrew Grannell expressed excitement and hope for a more "self-confident and generative phase" in the life of the school, he did not have to wait long to see a result. An opportunity presented itself immediately after he became dean in the summer of 1991. Bethany Theological Seminary, located not far from Chicago in Oak Brook, Illinois, had long been heading toward financial crisis. In 1990, the Bethany Board of Trustees made the decision to sell Bethany's building and property in the hopes of getting the school back on its feet. Bethany also decided to end several programs and cut back on the number of faculty and staff. In the spring of 1991, Wayne

Miller, Bethany's president, made it clear to the Board of Trustees that without other drastic cost-cutting measures, the school would have to close in 1994. Having used nearly all its assets and being deep in debt, Bethany decided to find more cost-effective ways of operating the school, such as through relocation and affiliation with another institution.

Affiliation was not a new possibility in Bethany's history. As a Church of the Brethren seminary, it had already "shared curriculum, faculty, and educational resources" with Mennonite Seminary from 1945–1958. Bethany had enrollment agreements with other Chicago seminaries, as well as shared a library with the nearby Northern Baptist Theological Seminary since 1963.[50] Oak Brook was the school's third location since its founding in 1905, so relocation was not a new part of Bethany's history, but moving out of the Chicago area was.

Relocation and affiliation were only two factors in the discussion when it came to Bethany's future. Of even more importance was the seminary's educational model. Originally be-

---

[50]Eugene Roop, "Affiliation of Bethany Theological Seminary: Financial Crisis and Educational Opportunity," 1-2, Andrew Grannell Papers, Friends Collection and Archives, Richmond, IN.

gun as Bethany Bible School, the school became Bethany Theological Seminary as a result of a more scholarly, academic curriculum in the 1960s and 1970s. The new model created a distance between the seminary and the larger Church of the Brethren, and the seminary began to fall out of touch with the needs of Brethren congregations. As the school looked into relocating elsewhere, some faculty members, Board members, and Bethany supporters also were hoping for a different model of education that would bring Bethany back to serving local congregations.[51]

Bethany considered a few seminaries for possible affiliation, including Associated Mennonite Biblical Seminary in Elkhart, Indiana; Christian Theological Seminary in Indianapolis; and United Theological Seminary in Dayton, Ohio. The site selection committee considered several criteria in looking at each school. Bethany wanted to retain its Church of the Brethren identity, remain an accredited institution, be a resource to and be informed by Church of the Brethren congregations, and to relocate to an urban area east of the Mississippi River but west of the Allegheny Mountains. Bethany also was looking for

---

[51] Eugene Roop, interview with author, 3-11-2009.

a school that would be willing to share costs, programs, library facilities, and some faculty and staff.[52] After two days of traveling to potential sites in Ohio and Indiana, the site committee concluded its tour by visiting a Quaker seminary in Richmond, Indiana.

When Bethany's site committee, which consisted of Henry Gibbel, Ruthann Knechel Johansen, Dean Fumitaka Matsuoka, and President Wayne Miller, scheduled a visit to ESR in spring 1991, it did not consider ESR to be high on the list of possible educational partners. Johansen, having had personal experience with Friends, suggested visiting ESR because it was along the travel route. When the group arrived, ESR's simple, meetinghouse-like structure spoke for itself: "This looks like home," one committee member commented, still standing in the parking lot. Interim Dean John Miller welcomed the site committee inside, gave a tour, and spent time explaining ESR's particular style of education. The more the committee heard, the more it liked. ESR's student-centered approach to education, Friends peace testimony, and no hierarchy in Friends'

---

[52]Eugene Roop, "Criteria for Relocation," in "Affiliation of Bethany Theological Seminary: Financial Crisis and Educational Opportunity," Appendix A, Grannell Papers; Wayne Miller, interview with author, 2-25-2009.

worship all pointed to a "spiritual companionship" between the two schools. ESR's genuine openness to exploring the possibility of partnership also appealed to the committee. "Something resonated" for everyone on the committee, Johansen remembered. They felt as though partnering with ESR could be a "comfortable kind of relationship."[53]

"ESR and Bethany's educational philosophies seemed to mesh well," Eugene Roop later commented. The two schools had similar ways of "conceiving a person's formation for ministry."[54] ESR also met other criteria for possible affiliation. Although Richmond was not a major city, Indianapolis and Dayton were about an hour's drive in either direction. Bethany was hoping to find new ways to promote the "life and needs" of Brethren congregations, and there were 58 Church of the Brethren congregations within 90 minutes of Richmond.[55] In July of 1991, Bethany's board received the site committee's recommendation to begin "serious" talks and negotiations with

---

[53]Ruthann Knechel Johansen, interview with author, 4-6-2009.

[54]Roop interview, 3-11-2009.

[55]"Bethany is on the Move ... Literally!," *Admissions Newsletter* of Bethany Theological Seminary, n.d., Cooper Papers.

ESR about possible partnership.[56] Then Wayne Miller, President of Bethany, telephoned Andrew Grannell to tell him of Bethany's intentions. Grannell received the call on his first day in the office as dean.

Forming the Partnership

Conversation between the two schools continued. ESR and Bethany had some definite similarities. Both schools were affiliated with historic peace churches and had emerged as dissenting voices to prevailing Christian tradition in Europe. Friends and Brethren were committed to living out their commitment to simplicity and peacemaking, and both groups "had a deep sense of the presence of Christ in the gathered community of faith." ESR was about the same size as Bethany and also served a fairly small denomination. The two schools even shared a Common Meal tradition, thanks to Eugene Roop, who liked ESR's Common Meal so much that he brought it to Bethany in 1978.

---

[56]William Kostlevy, *Bethany Theological Seminary: A Centennial History* (Richmond, IN: Bethany Theological Seminary and Brethren Journal Association, 2005), 176.

Definite differences also existed between the two schools. Friends emphasized the "moving of the Spirit" within the congregation more so than the Brethren, who had a preaching-centered worship. ESR tended to honor individual experience more and often used a Spirit-led process similar to group consensus to make decisions, rather than deciding by majority vote. The differences made it clear there would be no merger between ESR and Bethany, but rather a close partnership. This would allow each school to retain its respective denominational identity and particular style of decision-making and operation.[57]

Drawing on his previous experience in forming a joint peace studies program, Grannell saw several advantages for ESR in such a partnership. Because some of ESR's constituency questioned the school's Christian commitment, affiliating with Bethany might send a stronger and clearer message about ESR's Christian foundations and intentions. Even though ESR recognized a Friends model of pastoral ministry was different from the Church of the Brethren's, joining with Bethany might

---

[57]Roop, "Affiliation of Bethany Theological Seminary: Financial Crisis and Educational Opportunity," 6-7, Grannell Papers; Roop interview, 3-11-2009.

provide greater support for ESR's pastoral students. Since ESR valued the non-Quakers in its midst (having non-Quaker students at ESR had been a particular hope of Wil Cooper's), partnering with a Brethren institution would give the school an added layer of diversity. Both institutions were hoping for economic advantages through cost sharing, and ESR in particular hoped such cost-sharing might help to balance its budget, which had been running at a deficit.[58]

In 1992, Eugene Roop became Bethany's new president. As a Bethany professor, he was in favor of Bethany's new educational model, and he was very familiar with ESR, because he had taught Old Testament there during the 1970s. His becoming president made it very clear to Bethany supporters who preferred to stay in Chicago that a move to Richmond was probably imminent. By the end of the calendar year, Bethany's Board of Trustees committed the seminary to negotiating an affiliation agreement with ESR.

From 1992–1994, the two schools prepared for and formed the partnership. The presidents and deans of both in-

---

[58]Andrew Grannell, "Questions and Answers: ESR's Proposed Affiliation with Bethany," January 25, 1993, 4, Grannell Papers; Wil Cooper and Tom Mullen interview.

stitutions met regularly for discussions in Lafayette, Indiana because it was midway between Chicago and Richmond; Bethany's Board of Trustees and ESR's Board of Advisors went on a retreat together; each school's faculty met and spent time with one another. At the suggestion of ESR student Ken Jacobsen, Grannell asked George Kuh and Barbara Robinson, anthropologists of institutions at Indiana University, to perform a year-long cultural audit so the schools might be more aware of their differences and similarities. The Kuh-Robinson report examined the schools' different ways of understanding and responding to authority, worship, Christ, particular denominational structures, and styles of interaction and decision-making. The report also pointed out some of the major similarities, such as common understanding of living out beliefs or testimonies, as well as avoidance of creeds. In a report to the ESR community, Grannell and Jacobsen acknowledged that partnership with Bethany sounded risky with such different outward practices, even though the schools both had similar philosophical and spiritual visions and hopes. Grannell and Jacobsen also pointed out, however, that a true partnership could evolve through mutual understanding and supporting "critical parallels and balances." It was a risk, but it was also an opportunity.[59]

The Partnership

While both schools were excited about the ESR-Bethany partnership, there was also great deal of apprehension. ESR and Bethany were understandably cautious about the possibility of losing their respective denominational and institutional identities. ESR approached the partnership with measured optimism but also with some exhaustion. Some ESR faculty were not enthusiastic about preparing for the partnership because they were recovering from a series of community crises; they did not care for the extra committee work that went along with discerning and designing the partnership. ESR faculty also was wary of possibly giving up or changing a model of Quaker education for which they had experimented and worked hard to create.

Partnership and affiliation with a non-Quaker school was a relatively new step for ESR, although it had previous contact with other organizations and seminaries. In the 1970s

---

[59]Grannell, "Questions and Answers," 12.

and 1980s, ESR had been in networks with other seminaries in Ohio and Indiana, and this allowed for some cross-registration, joint fundraising, and ecumenical opportunities. The school had previous contacts and arrangements with Associated Mennonite Biblical Seminary and Bethany Theological Seminary related to peace studies, which had included a five-day biennial peace seminar in Washington, D.C.[60] ESR also had a close relationship with the small, Quaker-related Trueblood Academy for lay education since 1987 and enjoyed the benefits until 1992, when Jim Newby, its director, was called to other tasks. An "intentional, restrictive, and long term covenanting partnership" with Bethany was a new venture. Although both schools were careful not to use the marriage metaphor to describe what ESR and Bethany were doing (marriage implied merging and loss of identity), the partnership still had all the hard work and responsibilities that went along with a marriage. "It was like love at first sight," now-retired Bethany professor Murray Wagner said, remembering when the ESR and

---

[60] Cooper, *ESR Story*, 68, 90.

Bethany faculties first met. Everyone was starry-eyed until they later had to work out the details of their lives together.[61]

ESR made some changes to prepare for Bethany's arrival. Bethany planned to build literally next door to ESR, which meant Lawrence House, ESR's student housing building, had to be vacated. The College moved the house to College Avenue, where it was renamed Hole House. It now serves as theme housing for undergraduate students interested in the literary arts. ESR students who had resided in Lawrence House were sad to see it go, but expressed appreciation that ESR and Earlham College decided not to tear down the building. The students created a collage to commemorate Lawrence House, and the artwork is now included in ESR's archival collection at Lilly Library.

Bethany broke ground for its new building next to ESR's in summer 1993. By August 1994, the building was open and ready for the school year. The same month, ESR Dean Andrew Grannell, Bethany President Eugene Roop, and Earlham College President Richard Wood signed an agreement reflecting the outcomes of the ESR-Bethany discussions. The schools decided

---

[61]Grannell, "Questions and Answers," 4; Murray Wagner, interview with author, 3-11-2009.

to share student services, academic services, business management, and costs relating to Lilly Library. The schools also decided to coordinate their faculties. For example, ESR provides the Old Testament professor, and Bethany provides the New Testament professor. In this way, both schools share curriculum, although each retains its specific requirements. ESR and Bethany's partnership had officially begun.

ESR and Bethany: Fifteen Years Later

Fifteen years have passed since the deans and presidents set their hands to the initial affiliation agreement in 1994. Some things have changed, of course. ESR and Bethany no longer share student services and a business office, but they now share Information Technology staff and space. The schools still share a registrar, faculty coordination, and library costs. Students enjoy the opportunities for cross-registration at either school with no additional cost to them. Everyone agrees the expanded course offerings have been one of the greatest academic aspects of the partnership. "Educationally, it has been wonderful," Eugene Roop, now retired, says, and Jay Marshall, now ESR Dean, concurs, as does Lonnie Valentine, who has taught at ESR since 1989. ESR and Bethany jointly plan their course offerings, making sure each school offers courses specific to its denomination, faculty expertise, and student interests.

There have also been spiritual and ecumenical benefits to the partnership. ESR and Bethany have a weekly joint worship service and a monthly joint Common Meal. Students and the Peace Studies professors from both schools organize Peace Forum every week. Students walk in and out of each other's school buildings and go to classes together. They have formed meaningful friendships and have learned to appreciate the theological perspectives of each other's schools. At the same time, Friends and Brethren are sectarian, and occasionally students still become puzzled by the different cultural practices or theological understandings. Ruthann Knechel Johansen, Bethany's current president, feels the partnership is an "underdeveloped treasure" and hopes the two schools might live more deeply into their spiritual values and connection.[62]

From a financial perspective, ESR's partnership with Bethany has been less beneficial than ESR originally hoped, and from an administrative point of view, joint seminary com-

---

[62]Johansen interview, 4-6-2009.

mittees double the amount of time and energy needed from busy faculty and staff members. What keeps the ESR-Bethany partnership going is genuine, mutual respect and the desire and goodwill to make it work. The schools have things in common, but according to Roop, the differences really make the partnership work, not the similarities.[63] One instance of this is ESR and Bethany's shared commitment to peacemaking. The ways in which Friends and Brethren approach peacemaking, however, are different. Friends often take a more activist role in social justice and advocacy, whereas the Brethren see peacemaking as emerging from discipleship, or living like Jesus.[64] The shared commitments provide common ground, but the differences allow each school to retain its identity. "Being different" is how both institutions understand their denominational history, and it is how they often see themselves in relation to one another. At the same time, being different also is rooted in both schools' vision for living in the Kingdom of God. Undertaking the partnership, as Grannell acknowledged in 1994, was a risk, but it also became an opportunity for the

---

[63] Roop interview, 3-11-2009.

[64] Kostlevy, *Bethany Theological Seminary*, 196; Roop interview.

schools to learn from and strengthen each other. ESR and Bethany hope there may be many years of partnership to come.

CHAPTER FIVE:

ENTERING THE 21ST CENTURY

Finances

By the mid-1990s, ESR had taken steps to clarify its mission statement and to continue developing particularly Quaker aspects of the school's curriculum. With Bethany moved in next door, Grannell focused his attention on more external matters—specifically ESR's capital campaign. He and John Owen, ESR's Director of Development, spent significant time traveling and working with ESR's constituents during the final years of his deanship. ESR's finances, which were often tight, took a definite downturn in the early 1990s. The school was consistently running deficit budgets, which was a major cause for concern. ESR depended on three main sources of revenue: tuition, gifts to the Annual Fund, and the endowment. Tuition income was down because student enrollment decreased, and donations to the Annual Fund were down as well. Donors who pledged support for the Annual Fund during the previous campaign in the late 1980s fulfilled their pledges, but they did not "renew their giving to the Annual Fund at comparable levels." Several annual donors had also died, so ESR found itself struggling to meet the yearly costs of operation. Hoping to gain more support from the greater Society in the mid-1990s campaign, the school organized its efforts around the theme "An Investment in Friends Leadership." When the campaign came to an end in 1998, Grannell and Owen met and exceeded the $2.5 million goal.

The financial stress during this time was partially alleviated by the remarkable growth of the school's endowment. Between 1991 and 1998, the endowment more than doubled, thanks to the advice of Richard Smith, Earlham's Vice President of Financial Affairs, and the Earlham Foundation's management of the school's endowment funds. The endowment growth supported different aspects of the school's operation.

Leadership Changes and Repositioning

In 1997, Grannell announced his resignation effective June 30, 1998 to give ESR time to search for a replacement. Meanwhile, Earlham College was undergoing leadership changes of its own. Richard Wood ended his College presidency in 1996. After one year with an interim president, Earlham welcomed Douglas Bennett as the new president in 1997. Bennett was interested in looking closely at all the institutions then under the Earlham umbrella: Earlham College, ESR, and Conner Prairie. All three, he noticed, were having trouble with "audience"—the College was under-enrolled, as was the School of Religion, and Conner Prairie had very little earned income.[65] Bennett and the Earlham Board of Trustees decided to develop repositioning plans for all three institutions. In April 1997 the Board of Trustees appointed a Special Board Committee to study the main issues most urgent for ESR, which were governance, particular strategies for the school to "achieve fiscal equilibrium" with the continued budget deficits, and ways in which the school might best serve needs of the Religious Society of Friends.

---

[65]Douglas Bennett, interview with author, 3-12-2009.

In winter 1998, the Special Board Committee reported back to the Trustees on each of the main issues. Bennett presented a document addressing and clarifying ESR's governance structure. The new document spelled out the specific roles and responsibilities of each participant (Dean, Trustees, Advisors, faculty, students) in the school's governance, based on Earlham by-laws and ESR documents. Hoping to correct and reverse ESR's deficit pattern, the Special Board Committee suggested increasing enrollment, cutting administrative expenditures, and increasing gift-related income and annual giving. The increased enrollment and giving were contingent on the third, but very important, issue: a better relationship between ESR and the Religious Society of Friends.

In order to cultivate such an improved relationship, the Committee acted on the suggestion of ESR faculty, Board of Advisors, and Board of Trustees member Howard Mills by recommending a national consultation around the question, "How can Earlham School of Religion best serve the needs of the Religious Society of Friends?"[66] ESR had already thoughtfully con-

---

[66]Report of the Special Board Committee on ESR, Earlham Board of Trustees, Winter 1998; Earlham Board of Trustees Minutes, February 28, 1998.

considered school's identity and sense of mission, but now it was time to ask the larger Society what it needed, and how ESR could help. The Trustees approved the recommendation, but advised caution. ESR needed to be clear with Quakers across the country that the school could not solve the problems of the entire Religious Society of Friends.[67]

As ESR prepared to undertake the consultation, the school announced its next dean, Jay W. Marshall. Marshall, a North Carolina Friend who taught at ESR in 1990–1991 and was currently pastor of New Castle Friends Meeting, expressed excitement about taking on his new role. He recognized one of his immediate challenges as the upcoming national consultation, but he also hoped ESR would be a place where "Friends of all persuasions" might come to be better equipped for their particular calls to ministry. Some of ESR's constituents especially appreciated Marshall's pastoral experience in Indiana and North Carolina Yearly Meetings. *Quaker Life*, a Friends United Meeting publication, noted, "The appointment of Jay Marshall has been greeted as an indication that ESR intends to

---

[67]ESR Special Board Committee, Chair's Report, Earlham Board of Trustees, February 28, 1998.

strengthen its commitment to pastoral leadership for Friends in coming years."[68]

As his deanship ended, Andrew Grannell made plans to go to St. Johns University in Minnesota to research theological distance education. He left with a Minute of Appreciation from the Earlham Board of Trustees, thanking him for his work at ESR. Marshall became dean in the summer of 1998, and he joined Bennett in planning for the consultation.

Among Friends: A National Consultation

The ESR Board of Advisors, along with the help of a consulting company, Crane MetaMarketing Ltd., oversaw the consultation. ESR wanted to hear from Friends—young and old, evangelical and universalist, women and men, paid and unpaid leaders—from all over the country. What was the state of the Religious Society of Friends? What was the condition of Friends' leadership? Where did Friends think the Society was going? Based on answers to those questions, ESR wanted to know how Friends thought ESR could help the wider Society.

---

[68]"New dean excited to be at Earlham School of Religion," Richmond, IN *Palladium-Item*, April 25, 1998; "Jay Marshall Named Dean of ESR," *Quaker Life* (June 1998), 13; Jay Marshall correspondence, Wilmer Cooper Papers.

How might ESR prepare future leadership? What did Friends think of ESR and its graduates?

The Board of Advisors invited Friends in their yearly meetings to participate. Bennett and Marshall also spent time in conversation with Friends, asking them to recommend names of persons who might contribute to the discussion. Once Friends were invited, the Advisors formed 24 focus groups consisting of six to ten people that met in 22 locations throughout the United States. During the fall 1998 and the winter of 1999, the consultants attended each focus group session and conducted telephone interviews with individuals. ESR placed advertisements in *Friends Journal* and *Quaker Life*, encouraging Friends to write letters. In all, 255 Friends entered the discussion. Then Crane MetaMarketing prepared a final report based on the input from Friends in the consultation.[69]

During the fall of 1999, ESR faculty, the Board of Advisors, and the Earlham Board of Trustees received copies of the report. Overall, participants in the consultation felt the general Religious Society of Friends had lost its identity and no longer

---

[69]Douglas Bennett, "Request for Proposals, The Earlham School of Religion: A National Consultation," material from the Office of the Earlham President; *Among Friends: A consultation with Friends about the condition of Quakers in the U.S. today* (Richmond, IN: Earlham Press, 1999), 1–3.

knew what it stood for. There was too much in-fighting and division, the report said, and the Society was also out of touch with the outside world. The participants felt as though the Religious Society of Friends was stuck and did not know where it was going. Friends wanted leaders, but they also admitted Quakers often have trouble accepting authority. The report went on: Quaker pastoral ministry could be challenging, especially with low pay; at the same time, Friends knew anyone could lead. They did not always agree, however, on what leading meant. When it came to ESR, Friends had different understandings about which Friends ESR meant to serve and what the school's purpose was. Some thought ESR was evangelical, since it prepared pastors; others thought ESR was for unprogrammed Friends. Some participants were under the impression that ESR only prepared pastors, while others felt ESR did not prepare enough of them. Others said they really did not know much about ESR at all.

Yet the image of ESR as a meeting ground where growth and change took place emerged in Friends' conversations:

> I came out of an evangelical church and my roommate at ESR was from Pacific Yearly Meeting. He had books on Eastern spirituality and I had my books on the defense of the virgin birth. But we became great friends,

and he gained new appreciation for the Bible and I became a little less doctrinaire. That's the kind of thing that can happen at ESR at its best.

I went to ESR not knowing what to expect—and the diverse community there came as a shock. It forced me to discover for myself the Source of spiritual authority, not just accepting what I'd learned at Philadelphia Yearly Meeting.

What I like about ESR for unprogrammed Friends is that we went out there and were changed rather dramatically.... We got into the Bible and into disciplined theological reflection and we ended up, many of us, revising and deepening our understanding.[70]

Friends also identified ways ESR could help the larger Society. This included defining a new model of what Friends leadership looked like; ESR could prepare pastors *and* other types of leaders, such as clerks, teachers, and spiritual directors. Friends encouraged ESR to take a clear stand on what it was trying to do and to be "bold, creative, transformative." In addition, ESR would do well to be in touch with the larger Society by sending out information, being a resource to yearly meetings, making contacts with Friends nationally and interna-

---

[70]*Among Friends,* 49–50.

tionally, and creating and carrying out educational programs for Friends who were not residential students.[71]

The final report of the consultation was discouraging to some ESR faculty and staff. The school was not very visible to the broader Society; some Friends did not have a very clear sense of the school's mission, and other Friends formed their opinions of ESR based on misinformation or lack of knowledge. A few Friends were bitter in their assessment of the school: "There's *nothing* ESR could do to bring back the interest of my church. They asked me to tell you that."[72] At the same time, the news was not all bad. Friends recognized ESR as a crossroads where different kinds of Quakers interacted with each other, and they also thought the school had helped to foster better relations between different branches of Friends. Some students experienced significant spiritual transformation; others became friends with those whom they still disagreed. Friends in the consultation even pointed out ways they thought ESR had done a good job in training leadership:

> We have a lot of pastors here now who have been trained at ESR. And one of the reasons North Carolina

---

[71]Ibid., 55, 280–81.

[72]*Among Friends*, 48.

Yearly Meeting is so strong, so dynamic, is because there are so many fine young products of ESR down here.

Almost everywhere one looks today among unprogrammed Friends, one will find ESR alumni/ae.

As a group, the folks who graduated from ESR are a beacon of hope. They are sensible, often deeply reflective and well trained. The School has done, by and large, a great job in that regard.[73]

Strategic Planning

Crane suggested ESR make clear its institutional identity, improve the school's presence through increased contact with the larger Religious Society of Friends, and be a model in Quaker thought, scholarship, and practice. With the suggestions in mind, Bennett decided to keep the conversation going with Friends in the United States. Earlham Press published Crane's report as *Among Friends: A consultation with Friends about the condition of Quakers in the U.S. today.* Consultation participants received copies, as did clerks and superintendents of American yearly meetings. Summaries of the consultation also appeared in *Quaker Life* and *Friends Journal.* Bennett

---

[73]Ibid., 60–61.

wanted to hear the wider Society's reaction to the report, so ESR held discussion groups in California, Iowa, Pennsylvania, Ohio, and North Carolina.[74]

Marshall formed a committee consisting of two ESR faculty members, two Board of Advisors representatives, a student, and himself to develop a strategic plan for ESR's future. One of the specific tasks for the Strategic Planning Committee was to "think holistically about ESR and its mission." In response to Friends' sense that ESR was misunderstood and not well-known in the larger Society, the Committee suggested clarifying ESR's mission by making a few changes to the school's mission statement, mainly to emphasize ESR's Christian, Quaker position. The Committee turned to ESR's Credo, a statement of belief originally written by Wil Cooper: "We believe Christ is present, guiding and directing our lives, and that we can know and obey Christ's will." Out of this understanding, the Committee pointed out, came ESR's mission:

> Earlham School of Religion is a Christian graduate theological school in the Quaker tradition. ESR prepares

---

[74]*Among Friends*, 65; Memorandum from Douglas Bennett to ESR Board of Advisors and Earlham Board of Trustees, "Re: The National Consultation: An Overview of Next Steps," September 2, 1999, material from the Office of the Earlham President.

women and men for leadership that empowers and for ministry that serves. This mission grows out of our Christian belief that God calls everyone to ministry. Using a transformative model of education, ESR encourages students to explore the intellectual, spiritual, and practical dimensions of their calls to ministry.[75]

The Committee also considered ESR's "audience." Knowing ESR could not realistically serve the entire Friends theological spectrum, the Committee decided to aim for the center. Although all Friends are certainly welcome to come to the school, ESR acknowledges it "best serves those who fall within a range of 'progressive evangelical' and 'confessing liberal' in the Christian tradition." *Progressive evangelical* refers to those who hold traditional Christian beliefs but are willing to learn and interact with others who may believe differently. *Confessing liberal* applies to those who do not hold traditional beliefs, but nevertheless still consider themselves part of the Body of Christ.[76] This is now printed in ESR catalogs and appears in admissions brochures and materials.

In the spring of 2000, the Committee approved the final version of the Strategic Plan, which proposed concrete ways

---

[75]Earlham School of Religion Strategic Plan, May 4, 2000 in *Self-Study Report for the Association of Theological Schools* (2006), Appendix 5, 3.

[76]ESR *Catalog* (2007–2009), 4.

for ESR to improve recruitment, fundraising, and connections with the wider Society. Some of these included increased Internet presence, hosting events around the country, and regularly visiting yearly meetings or Friends conferences. One of the Strategic Plan's proposals called in particular for an "experiment in extending ESR's reach and presence" by implementing a distance education program.[77] This program, which would allow students to work toward a Master of Divinity/Ministry degree without having to relocate to Richmond, became known as *ESR Access*.

Technology in Education at ESR

When ESR began as a small graduate program housed in Earlham College's Carpenter Hall, using computers as a common educational tool was beyond anyone's imagination. In fact, computer use among the faculty and staff was only starting to take off around the time the ESR building was being built. After moving into the renovated Robert Barclay Center in 1989, faculty and staff used computers regularly for word processing. The new ESR building came with space specifically set aside for

---

[77]Strategic Plan, May 4, 2000 in *Self-Study Report for the Association of Theological Schools* (2006), Appendix 5, 8.

student computer labs, and not long after the building opened, a gift helped the school purchase 12 Macintosh computers for student use. Andrew Grannell was particularly interested in bringing the school's technology up to date, and during his deanship, ESR laid a cable connecting the seminary to Earlham's computing system. When Grannell's time as dean ended, the Earlham Board of Trustees thanked him for his contribution to ESR's technology, recognizing it "will be felt for years to come." Although ESR and the College now maintain separate computing networks, Grannell's choice to connect the two was an important decision that brought ESR into the "technological world."[78]

In 1998, the school hired Stephen Spyker, a 1995 ESR graduate, as Director of Information Technology. Zach Noffsinger Erbaugh, employed by Bethany, joined the IT staff in 2000. He eventually became Network Services Manager for Seminary Computing Services (SCS), which serves ESR and Bethany. Deeply interested in the relationship between spirituality and technology, Spyker encouraged more sustainable buying practices, as well as the use of open-source software. In

---

[78]Minute of Appreciation for Andrew Grannell, Earlham Board of Trustees Minutes, June 6, 1998.

open-source, the programming code is available to anyone who wishes to use it or change it. In other types of software, makers carefully guard the code, and access to it is expensive. Spyker saw open-source as a more ethical and cost-effective option for the seminaries.[79] SCS continues to use open-source alongside more traditional software. After Spyker left in 2005, Erbaugh became Director.

Distance Education and *ESR Access*

Although technology enabling 21st century-style distance education was not available to ESR in the 1960s, ESR was interested in distance education very early on with extension courses in Indianapolis and Fairmount, Indiana. In more recent years, ESR offered intensive courses at regional sites in the United States, such as North Carolina, Iowa, Connecticut, and California. Owing to lack of interest, this aspect of distance education was discontinued.

As early as 1992, Keith Esch reported to the Earlham Board of Trustees that relocation to Richmond kept some po-

---

[79]Steve Spyker, "Report from the Director of Information Technology," ESR Board of Advisors, September 5, 2003, H–3.

tential students from applying to ESR.[80] As a result of the 1998 consultation, the school began to think about distance education as one way to reach students outside of Richmond. Thanks to a grant from the Lilly Foundation, ESR faculty learned more about incorporating technology with "pedagogical strategies." The grant was not for developing distance education, but the skills and experience the faculty gained through the grant prepared them for *ESR Access*, which was launched in 2001 and today accounts for nearly one half of ESR's enrollment. ESR also created a new Associate Dean of Distributed Learning position and hired Timothy Seid in 2001. He works with ESR faculty to design courses for online formats and oversees the distance education program.[81]

ESR Access is an online learning program that allows students to take courses and/or complete a degree without having to relocate to Richmond. Since community is an important aspect of an ESR education, the program includes two-week intensives on site in Richmond. During those intensives, *ESR Access* students interact with the residential ESR commu-

---

[80]Recruitment Planning Report: Earlham School of Religion, Earlham Board of Trustees, February 17, 1992, 73, 76.

[81]*Self-Study Report for the Association of Theological Schools* (2006), 60.

nity through Common Meals, worship, and the classroom. Although they make meaningful connections with each other through online courses, intensives are especially joyful and exciting times for distance learning students because they can see and talk to some of their online classmates in person.

The first *ESR Access* class graduated in May 2007. Besides being a significant achievement in distance education for ESR, the 2007 class was also an accomplishment in international distance education. Class member Julia Ryberg completed her degree while residing in Sweden. Other students in the class were from New York, Michigan, and Maryland. The entire distance learning graduating class joined the residential students for graduation activities and received their degrees at Earlham's Commencement.

Beginning the *ESR Access* program in 2001, like founding ESR in 1960, was something new and risky. There was no guarantee the new offering would work, and the nature of distance education drew criticism and doubt. "How can the distance learning model be effective, especially in ministry?" some people wondered. "Where is interaction with community in online education?" These are important questions, and ESR continues to struggle with them. Yet *ESR Access* plays an important role in the lives of students who live far away from Richmond. "We can't help that we were called to ministry at this time in our lives," Michael Fales pointed out on behalf of his classmates shortly before graduation in 2007. "We're just glad ESR has this program so we can be faithful to our call." Fales himself experienced a call to ministry at age 50. He lived in Michigan, had a family, and was employed full time. Because of *ESR Access*, he was able to complete a degree at an accredited institution without major life changes. Fales is Director of Service Learning and Campus Ministries at Olivet College in Michigan and was recently appointed as Assistant Professor of Interdisciplinary Studies and Religion.[82]

The *Among Friends* consultation in 1998–1999 bore similarities to the feasibility study Wil Cooper conducted in 1959. Both involved traveling and talking with Friends all over the country, and both determined the direction ESR would take. Cooper's study resulted in an experimental program that eventually became a full-fledged seminary for training pastoral ministers and others for Friends leadership. The consultation empowered ESR—a seminary serving a divided denomina-

---

[82]Michael Fales, e-mail message to author, 3-4-2009.

tion—to make a clear statement about the school's Christian, Quaker identity. ESR also made a conscious decision to serve students in the broad center of the wider Religious Society of Friends. The consultation also gave rise to *ESR Access*. In 1998, when ESR committed to "listening carefully to what Friends across the country have to say," the school meant it. The wider Society wanted ESR to be more available, more present, and ESR took steps to do that, one of which was implementing distance education to reach more people at a geographic distance. *ESR Access*, like ESR itself, was a bold, adventuresome experiment in theological education, both for the school and for the students involved. But then again, living in the Spirit always has been a bold and adventuresome task.

When Board of Trustees member Howard Mills urged ESR to conduct nationwide consultation with Friends, he recognized the relationship between the school of religion and the wider Society. ESR embodies some of the Society's hurtful divisions over theology and the nature of ministry, but the school also carries within itself the Society's best gifts: incredible Christ-rooted power and energy for change. As ESR approaches its 50th year, the school continues to prepare transformed, empowered leaders within the Religious Society of Friends.

CHAPTER SIX:

PREPARING FOR MINISTRY IN THE 21ST CENTURY

As ESR seeks to prepare Friends leadership and ministers for the 21st century, the school finds itself in an increas-
ingly complex and interconnected world. ESR attracts a diverse
group of Friends, and so the school has likewise developed a
diverse curriculum that encourages cross-cultural engagement,
spiritual grounding, and enlightened thinking. Although students have specific required courses, both the Master of Divin-
ity/Ministry and the Master of Arts in Religion degrees allow
ample room for a specific area of concentration based on the
student's interests and call to ministry. In addition to educational training, ESR serves the broader Religious Society of

Friends through the work of alumni/ae, as well as through pro-grams designed to strengthen the Society at the monthly meet-ing level.

Pastoral Ministry

Both Indiana and Western Yearly Meetings had been doubtful about ESR's interest in pastoral ministry in the early to mid-1990s. When Jay Marshall became dean, programmed Friends saw ESR clearly demonstrating its commitment to training pastoral ministers. In the fall of 1998, ESR hosted its first annual Pastors Conference, which included seasoned Friends pastors as speakers. This event, which has since fea-tured speakers engaging evangelism, spirituality, and preach-ing, is open to the community. Friends United Meeting spon-sored a second conference in winter 1999 at ESR, which exam-ined "practical aspects of pastoral ministry among Friends." The fall 1999 issue of *ESR Reports* published a conversation among five ESR graduates who were currently pastors: David Brindle (1980), Rex Jones (1985), Phil King (1985), Karen Mendenhall (1993), and Deborah Seuss (1991).[83]

---

[83]Dean's Report, ESR Board of Advisors, September 1998, A2; Brent Bill, "'Not Always Easy, But Good': Five ESR Grads Talk About Pastoral Ministry,"

The task of finding and hiring a permanent professor of pastoral studies had been underway for a few years. Tom Mullen taught courses in pastoral ministry before his retirement in 1990, and he developed a course called Work of the Pastor, a class now taken by many students with a pastoral ministry emphasis. When Mullen retired from the deanship, he continued to teach preaching, and Joshua Brown, a 1984 graduate and pastor of West Richmond Friends Meeting, took over teaching Work of the Pastor. In 1999, Philip Baisley, 1993 ESR alum and pastor at Williamsburg Friends Meeting, became Assistant Professor of Pastoral Studies. He has developed several courses of his own, including Pastoral Spirituality, The Friends Pastor, and The Pastor and Religious Education. He also reinvented other courses already in ESR's catalog, such as The Church's Mission in a World Community, and Theology and Preaching. Baisley also coordinates the annual Pastors Conference. Recent ESR graduates who serve as pastoral ministers include April Vanlonden (2004), Chris Sitler (2006), Jeff Wolfe (2007), and Brian Young (2009).

ESR Reports (Fall 1999), 1–3.

Supervised Ministry

In 1997, Ann Miller resigned her position as Director of Field Education to become Associate Professor of Spirituality after national searches failed to find a replacement for Margaret Benefiel, the previous professor. Several people provided interim directorship for Field Education, including Keith Esch and Jim Bower. Stephanie Crumley-Effinger, 1981 ESR graduate and former Earlham College campus minister, joined the ESR faculty as Director of Field Education in 2000. While retaining much of Ann Miller's design for Discernment and Call of Gifts for Ministry, Crumley-Effinger opened field education possibilities even further by introducing a project-based internship option, which allowed students who felt calls to writing or other artistic expression to work on a specific project, rather than be limited to a site-based field education internship. ESR is committed to gifts-based ministry, believing students should not be funneled into ministry to which they do not feel called. The site or project also should be one of the students' choosing, not a faculty decision.

ESR students have worked in a variety of projects and settings, such as youth ministry at St. Luke's Methodist Church in Indianapolis; pastoral internships at Friends meetings in or near Richmond; mediation and restorative practices at Richmond's Conflict Resolution Center; hospital, retirement community, and hospice chaplaincy; teaching writing and poetry at Richmond Friends School; teaching assistantships at Earlham College; prison ministry; bringing out unheard voices through teaching creative writing and music in Ramallah, Palestine; spiritual directorships; body work; group facilitation; research and writing. Supervised Ministry sites or projects at ESR tend to be creative and are designed to fit the individual student's call, needs, and interests.

A very noticeable surface change to the Field Education for Ministry Seminar and experience at ESR is nomenclature. Throughout most of the school's history, students did a Ministry Project in their final year, but in 1992, the name was changed to Field Education for Ministry after a faculty review of the program. Most recently in 2007, Field Education became Supervised Ministry. Not only is the new term less confusing, it is "more descriptive," which is, as Crumley-Effinger explained, more "appropriate for a 'plain-speaking' Quaker seminary to use."[84]

---

[84]Stephanie Crumley-Effinger, e-mail message to author, 11-24-2008.

Cross Cultural Education

In 1986, Wil Cooper observed, "The most rapidly growing Meetings within Quakerism today are found in Third World countries. There also are several newly formed ethnic Meetings in the USA." He thought ESR should invite more "spokespersons and leaders from Third World Quakerism" to visit the school, and ESR should also do more to send students and faculty to Third World countries as well as to interact with ethnic people in the United States. In general, he noted, "we need to be more intentional about including a global perspective in our curriculum."[85] This was an opinion shared by theology professor and Interim Dean John Miller in the early 1990s.

For the next few years, ESR participated in a variety in cross-cultural experiences. In 1989, for example, students "gave a van to Belize Council of Churches ... and drove it there." The following year, the ESR faculty went to the Central American country of Belize. They spent time there working with Sadie Vernon (1976), who started what later became the Belize Friends Boys School. During the early 1990s, there were two student seminars to El Salvador, and one faculty member stud-

---

[85] *ATS Accreditation Self-Study* (1986), 14–15.

ied Spanish in Guatemala for a summer and then visited Quakers in Mexico and Cuba. Cross-cultural activity was not limited to the Americas. One faculty member spent the 1995 fall semester in Jerusalem. Faculty member Bill Ratliff spent a sabbatical year as Resident Scholar at Pacific Theological College on the Fiji Islands. As a result of that and other visits, ESR and Pacific Theological College made a student exchange. Three PTC students came to ESR for a term in 1995, and a few ESR students studied at PTC for a term in 1996.[86]

ESR has begun to think even more seriously about cross-cultural engagement. In 2006, the ESR faculty, with Manuel Guzman (1996) serving as translator, traveled to Honduras to meet with Friends there and spent considerable time learning Spanish at an intensive language school. This inspired David Johns, Associate Professor of Theology, to spend part of his sabbatical teaching theology at the Colegio Biblico Jorge Fox in Honduras. He also was Friend-in-Residence at Casa de los Amigos in Mexico City for the summer of 2008. Susan Yanos, Assistant Professor of Writing, also traveled to Nicaragua

---

[86]"ESR Participation in Cross-Cultural Experiences (1986–95)," in *Self-Study Report for Accreditation Review* (1996), Appendix H; Board of Advisors Minutes, November 4-6, 1995, 38.

and taught a two-week writing course there. ESR invited Reverend José Miguel Torres, assistant director of Instituto de Investigaciones y Acción Social at the Martin Luther King Universidad Politécnica de Nicaragua, to be the Willson Lecturer in 2007. He delivered the lecture entirely in Spanish, with former and then-current ESR students Dinora Uvalle (1998), Adriana Cabrera (2008), and Micah Bales (2009) providing translation.

Students also are engaging cross-culturally. Elisabeth Beasley, a 2007 graduate, received funding to study in Tanzania for the fall of 2006. She spent one of her three months abroad at Friends Theological College (FTC) in Kaimosi, Kenya. Her visit occurred at the same time Benson Khamasi Amugamwa, a teacher at FTC, was on study leave to obtain a Master of Arts degree at ESR. Margaret Hawthorn, a 2008 graduate, completed part of her Supervised Ministry project in Ramallah, Palestine. Bethany Theological Seminary has a cross-cultural requirement for degree programs, and some ESR students have participated in Bethany's travel seminars. ESR recently added a cross-cultural component of its own. Students may travel abroad, or they may choose to spend time in an unfamiliar cultural setting in the United States. Given the multicultural world of the 21st century, ESR now also offers a course in interfaith understanding, called Christianity and the World's Faiths. This class examines particular Christian visions and responses to religious diversity.[87]

Diversity at ESR

In 1985, ESR did not attract many African American[88] or international students, although there had been greater diversity in the school's earlier years. The international students who came to ESR in the school's early years most often were from Europe, Africa, and Asia. Since the mid- to late 1990s, more students have come from Latin American countries, such as Mexico and Colombia. In the past ten years, ESR has welcomed residential students coming from Kenya, Rwanda, South Korea, Lithuania, the United Kingdom, Germany, Mexico, Colombia, and Canada. *ESR Access* students have been from Denmark, Guatemala, Kenya, and Sweden. Many of these students come from Friends meetings in their respective countries and

---

[87]ESR *Catalog* (2007–2009), 48.

[88]The Religious Society of Friends as whole has never had a large African American population, despite the Society's abolitionist stance in the late 19th century.

bring cultural and theological perspectives that both challenge and enrich other students and faculty at the school.

More than 50 percent of all residential and *ESR Access* students identify as Friends. During the 2006–2007 school year, ESR's student body represented 24 yearly meetings from the United States and around the world. The numbers of students from Friends United Meeting and Friends General Conference were equal, and several students came from yearly meetings affiliated with both organizations. A few ESR students came from independent yearly meetings, a small number of students represented Conservative yearly meetings, and five students represented yearly meetings in South America, Africa, and Europe. Of the nine regular faculty members, four hold membership in other churches, and the rest represent both programmed and unprogrammed Friends traditions. ESR is a very cosmopolitan place when it comes to diversity among Friends.[89]

A little less than 50 percent of ESR students come from denominational backgrounds other than Quaker. A few stu-

---

[89]"Source of ESR Students by Yearly Meeting, 2006-2007," material from the Office of the ESR Dean; information supplied by Seminary Academic Services, Office of the Registrar.

dents come from the Church of the Brethren, and there is some representation from mainline denominations such as Roman Catholicism, Anglican/Episcopalian, and Presbyterian. A small number of Pentecostal and non-denominational students also have attended, including one student from a Vineyard church. From 2004–2008, non-Friends denominations with the highest number of students at ESR were United Church of Christ, United Methodist, and Unitarian Universalist.[90] Some non-Quaker students come to ESR because the school offers courses that fit their career goals; others come because of ESR's reasonable tuition; and others come because ESR's open, spiritual atmosphere appeals to them. Suzanne LeVesconte (2009) was studying for ordination in the Episcopal Church. Drawn to ESR because of the school's emphasis on discernment and spiritual formation, LeVesconte asked her bishop if she could finish her Master of Divinity studies at ESR. The bishop agreed, which meant LeVesconte delayed her plans by one or two years to transfer to an Episcopal seminary for study in liturgy. "But it was important," LeVesconte wrote, "for me to finish the proc-

---

[90]"ATS Enrollment by Denomination, 2004-2008," material from the Office of the ESR Dean; information supplied by Seminary Academic Services, Office of the Registrar.

ess of ... formation that I had started at ESR."[91] The school plays a role in preparing Friends for ministry, but also preparing grounded, Spirit-led ministers in the larger Church.

Scholarship

Most ESR students enroll in the Master of Divinity/Ministry program, which includes Supervised Ministry as part of the requirement for the degree. A smaller number of students enter the Master of Arts in Religion program, which requires a thesis instead of Supervised Ministry. Students have written on a variety of topics that fall under four categories: Biblical Studies, Christian Theological Studies, Peace and Justice Studies, and Quaker Studies. Thesis titles over the past 25 years include:

> *Gospel order among quietist Quakers in the nineteenth century to 1860: a comparison of the Hicksite and Wilburite understandings of the discipline*
>
> *Gentle invaders: Quaker women educators and race during the Civil War and reconstruction*[92]

---

[91]Suzanne LeVesconte, e-mail message to the author, 2-6-2009.

[92]Linda B. Selleck, the writer of this thesis, eventually developed her work into book form. It was published in 1995.

Paul and Fox on the road to Damascus: sent to turn people to the light

God and the world: a process theology's reflection on the relationship of God to the biodiversity crisis and humanity

Non-Violent action versus temptation to leave the Holy land: a Palestinian Christian perspective

The covenant faithfulness of Jesus the messiah: a narrative theology of obedience and nonviolence, particularity and credibility

In addition to research and writing, M.A. students must also pass an oral examination of their topic to receive a degree. This program best serves students who have interest in doctoral education, teaching, or even faith-based service organizations.[93] All degree-seeking students must take courses in Old Testament, New Testament, history of Christianity, and theology, and students learn and sharpen their skills in Biblical exegesis, historical research, and writing. ESR values and encourages intellectual work in preparation for ministry.

---

[93]Sulek, *Case for Support*, C–11.

Students have many resources available to them for intellectual preparation. In 2003, ESR developed the Digital Quaker Collection, an online resource for researching 17th- and 18th-century Quaker texts. The Collection, which contains over 500 works, allows students and non-student researchers to enter names, keywords, and dates in order to find specific texts or a particular topic discussed in a number of texts. In addition to this online resource, ESR students also have access to the Friends Collection and Archives located in Lilly Library on the Earlham College campus. The Collection contains several thousand volumes on Quaker history, biography, theology, and literature, as well as resources in Friends genealogy. The collection also receives a number of Quaker periodicals. The Archives collection houses papers, books, and photographs from Indiana and Western Yearly Meetings and Friends United Meeting, as well as holds College and ESR historical records. It also has over 400 manuscript collections. Lilly Library has a substantial collection of theological books and electronic journal subscriptions, as well as a theological librarian, who works with both faculty and students at ESR and Bethany.[94]

---

[94]*Self-Study Report for the Association of Theological Schools* (2006), 41.

Quaker scholarship is important to ESR faculty and alumni/ae, in keeping with the school's goal to be a model in Quaker theological education, scholarship, and thought. Stephen Angell, a 1982 ESR alum who became Geraldine Leatherock Professor of Quaker Studies after John Punshon's retirement in 2001, recently co-edited *Quaker Bible Reader* with Paul Buckley (2001). Published by ESR, the book features essays written by different Friends on how they interpret the Scriptures. Angell also served as an editor of *Quaker Theology*, and Buckley has translated works of William Penn into modern-day English in his book, *Twenty-First Century Penn*. Michael Birkel (1979) and Mary Garman (1977), both Earlham College professors who teach courses at ESR, have contributed to the realm of Quaker scholarship through Birkel's *Engaging Scripture: Reading the Bible with Early Friends*, among other works, and Garman's *Hidden in Plain Sight: Quaker Women's Writings, 1650–1700*. David Johns (1989) is Associate Professor of Theology at ESR and is an editorial advisor to *Quaker Religious Thought*, published by the Quaker Theological Discussion Group. Paul Anderson (1981), professor of Biblical and Quaker Studies at George Fox University, has served as editor of *Evangelical Friend* and is currently the editor of *Quaker Religious*

Thought. ESR also publishes resources for Friends meetings and churches, such as *Leading Friends* by Jennifer Isbell (2007) and *Where the Wind Blows: Vitality Among Friends* by Jay Marshall.

ESR faculty and alumni/ae are active in other areas of research and scholarship. Nancy Bowen, Associate Professor of Old Testament, is under contract to write a volume on Ezekiel for *Old Testament Commentaries* published by Abingdon Press. After Matt Hisrich graduated in 2008, he attended the Second International Conference of the Austrian School of Economics in the 21st Century, which was held in Argentina. There he presented a paper that related economics to "certain theological assumptions" and proposed a more "other-directed approach that would seek out what the experiences and insights our neighbors might have to offer to economic understanding." Some attendees liked the proposal and later engaged Hisrich in further conversation.[95] Hisrich continues to do ministry related to faith and finances; he is now Indiana Yearly Meeting's Ministerial Advocate, a person who works with Friends meetings

---

[95]Matt Hisrich, "Exploring Faith & Economics in Argentina," *ESR Reports* (Fall 2008), 6.

and pastors to help alleviate economic challenges faced by many pastoral leaders.

Ministry of Writing

In addition to ministry through scholarship, ESR recognizes ministry through literary and spiritual writing. Early Friends were known as "publishers of truth" because of their written tracts, pamphlets, and journals, and ESR considers its Ministry of Writing program as continuing the Friends tradition of ministry through the written word. The program at Earlham School of Religion had its beginnings in 1984, when Tom Mullen taught a course called Writing for the Religious Market. Mullen rightly pointed out, however, that the ministry of writing actually started when ESR students began to publish books. Drawn to the teaching of professor and writer Elton Trueblood, a student named Keith Miller finished a degree at ESR in 1964. He published the popular *A Taste of New Wine* in 1966[96] and went on to write several more books. Miller would

---

[96]Mullen interview, 10-27-2008.

later write that ESR gave him "an excellent base from which to try to do the ministry I feel called to—that of writing."[97]

Mullen continued to teach writing after his retirement in 1990. He saw writing courses as a way not only to encourage and train those who felt called specifically to writing as ministry, but also to aid others who might be called to other types of ministry—pastoral ministry, spirituality, or peace and justice work—to write sermons or devotional articles. In 1992 Mullen developed a plan for the future writing emphasis, which included a course sequence, ideas for Supervised Ministry projects, and workshops. The requirements for the present-day writing emphasis bear similarity to Mullen's original ideas.

The Ministry of Writing Colloquium was established in honor of Tom Mullen's retirement from the deanship in 1990. The Colloquium, which features a speaker and several workshops, has been held annually since 1992. The keynote speakers are writers, some of whom are known to broader audiences, such as Madeleine L'Engle, Donna Jo Napoli, Robert Olen Butler, and Elizabeth Dewberry. Other writers are readily recognized among Indiana Quaker audiences, such as Scott Russell

---

[97] Cooper, *ESR Story*, 113.

Sanders, Phil Gulley, and Haven Kimmel, whose 2002 memoir *A Girl Named Zippy* began as a draft in one of Mullen's classes during the 1990s. ESR has hosted poets Li-Young Lee and Diane Glancy, as well as writers known to the Christian publishing world, such as Lauren Winner. Lil Copan, editor at Paraclete Press, frequently presented workshops at the Colloquium. This gathering of writers draws attendees nationwide, and the Colloquium's small bookstore often includes books published by ESR graduates, such as Steven Cleaver (2004) and Donne Hayden (2006).

After Tom Mullen stopped teaching writing courses in 1997, part-time instructors continued the task, including former students Brent Bill (1980) and Peter Anderson (2001), and Barbara Mays, former editor of Friends United Press. In 2006, ESR hired Susan Yanos as Assistant Professor and Director of the Mullen Ministry of Writing Program. Yanos, who came with background as an English professor, redesigned several writing courses and reinvented others. She also has encouraged students to share their writing in venues outside the school.

In addition to the annual Colloquium, the Ministry of Writing program offers a one-year, non-degree W.O.R.D. Sojourn for students who would like to explore writing as ministry without commitment to a Master of Divinity degree. ESR also offers the Mullen Ministry of Writing Fellowship, a fellowship that grants the recipient time, $1,500, and space to work on a significant writing project. Several students have received this fellowship, including current students Katie Terrell and Julia Pantoga.

Christian Spirituality

Attending to the Spirit's movement and leading is a central part of Friends' spirituality. All Master of Divinity/Ministry students take Spiritual Preparation for Ministry, and some students choose a ministry emphasis in spirituality. They often minister to their fellow classmates, who gratefully attend writing workshops or quiet springtime retreats led by spirituality students. Many graduate with experience in giving individual spiritual direction, as well as with guided practice in prayer and spiritual disciplines. These students have gone on to a variety of jobs and careers, including chaplaincy, pastoral ministry, healing and bodywork, retreat ministry, and spiritual directorships. In 2006, several students graduated with a Spirituality emphasis, attesting to its present relevance both to the

Religious Society of Friends and to the larger Body of Christ. ESR's Spirituality program influence has gone as far away as Lithuania, where Violeta Tribandiene (2002) transported a canvas labyrinth made by Carol Sexton (2001) and the ESR community. Tribandiene encouraged her fellow Lithuanians to walk the labyrinth and to write their thoughts in the labyrinth journal. "I am impressed by the beauty of the sharings," wrote Tribandiene. The journal recorded experiences of "Forgiveness, power of creation, direct contact with the Christ within, and ever-present spiritual nurture."[98]

Ann Miller, who was Associate Professor of Spirituality from 1997–2000, developed, redesigned, and taught courses still offered today: Individual Spiritual Direction, Group Spiritual Direction, and Prayer. She also taught Christian Discipleship and Living in the Spirit, as well as Feminist Spirituality. After Miller retired, Stephanie Ford joined ESR's faculty as Assistant Professor of Spirituality. She designed two new courses, Spirituality and the Arts and Spirituality and the Body, the latter drawing high enrollment when it is offered. Ford also created the annual Spirituality Gathering. This day-long event has

---

[98]Violeta Tribandiene, "ESR in Lithuania," *ESR Reports* (Fall 2006), 5.

keynote speakers and workshops related to a specific theme. Previous events have included Praying with Our Bodies (2004), Listening to the Heart of Music (2005) with Fran McKendree as speaker, Spirituality and Ecology (2006) with Keith Helmuth, The Healing Power of Prayer (2007), Seeking Simplicity (2008) with Catherine Whitmire, and Listening to the Spirit (2009). Many attendees come from Ohio and Indiana.[99]

Pastoral Care

Pastoral care is another area in which ESR prepares students for ministry. Students interested in pastoral ministry in a congregational setting often take these courses, as well. This ministry emphasis focuses on helping students gain a sense of self-awareness, as well as specific theological and clinical tools as they minister to others. Graduating pastoral care students are prepared to enter training programs that "may lead to certification as a chaplain or a pastoral counselor."[100] Alumni/ae with this ministry emphasis often enter

---

[99] *Self-Study Report for the Association of Theological Schools* (2006), 34–35, 36–37.

[100] ESR *Catalog* (2007–2009), 24.

year-long units of Clinical Pastoral Education in hospitals or mental health facilities. Keith Dobyns (1998) was particularly concerned for the spiritual care of those in medical training and co-developed the Program for Integration of Spirituality in Medicine (PRISM) at Kettering (Ohio) Network Hospitals. This program encourages medical students and residents to recognize that their own spirituality can have an effect on the well-being of their patients.[101]

ESR benefited greatly from the gentle expertise of Bill Ratliff, Professor of Pastoral Care and Counseling, who came to ESR in 1985. He was the first faculty member at ESR to have special and specific training in pastoral care and counseling. During his 18 years at ESR, Ratliff designed courses for the pastoral care ministry emphasis, including Emergency Pastoral Care and Creative Use of Anger in Ministry. Beginning in 1991, Ratliff organized the Quakers in Pastoral Care and Counseling conference, which ESR hosted several times before it moved to the Quaker Hill Conference Center. Ratliff retired in 2003, and Jim Higginbotham joined the ESR faculty as Assistant Professor of Pastoral Care and Counseling in 2005. Higginbotham came

---

[101]Keith Dobyns, "The PRISM Project," *ESR Reports* (Fall 2001), 4–5.

with experience in pastoral ministry, pastoral counseling, and chaplaincy, and he has since redesigned the Pastoral Care with Family Systems course so that it could be offered online.[102]

Helping Students Prepare for Ministry

As ESR students attend classes, go to Common Meal and worship, puzzle out their calls to ministry, and wrestle with writing their credos for Constructive Theology, considerable work is going on behind the scenes to keep the school running. The faculty go to business meetings, read and evaluate student papers, and prepare for classes. They meet with Bethany faculty to determine course offerings for the following year; they work on their own scholarship and professional development. One day the Dean might be writing a report to the Board of Trustees, because ESR is financially and legally responsible in all ways to this body, and another day he might be presenting a "State of the Seminary" overview for the Common Meal program. The Assistant to the Dean organizes material for the next meeting of the Board of Advisors, a group of Friends that literally advises ESR in administrative and financial matters. The

---

[102]*Self-Study Report for the Association of Theological Schools* (2006), 34.

Advisors also are a "channel of communication, in both directions, between the Earlham School of Religion and the wider world of Friends."[103] More goes into ministry preparation than students simply going to class.

Meanwhile, the Director of Admissions responds to e-mail inquiries and gets ready to travel to a peace conference in order to set up a table with ESR brochures and viewbooks, and the Director of External Relations invites Friends and alumnae to donate to ESR's Annual Fund. As the custodian consults the Business Manager on how to make sure the thermostats keep the ESR building at the right temperature, the Business Manager is also carefully preparing financial aid packages for returning students the following year. While this is happening, the Director of Outreach leads a workshop in Philadelphia on Friends leadership and suggests ways ESR could be a resource to monthly meetings. The receptionist welcomes a prospective student, and staff from Computer Services is busy unjamming paper in the computer lab printer as a student looks on, anxiously feeling time move closer to the start of class.

---

[103]Ibid., "Governance of ESR," Appendix 4.

ESR relies on tuition, the endowment, and gifts to provide space, expertise, and training for future Friends leadership. Marty Sulek, ESR's Director of Development from 2003–2005, developed a *Case for Support* that encourages donors to give to specific programs, such as pastoral ministry or spirituality, because the traditional campaign model with Earlham College does not meet ESR's needs. A campaign does not always engage the people ESR wants to serve—that is, the Religious Society of Friends. ESR hopes donors will give from a sense of spiritual generosity, and so the school wants to "pursue thoughtful conversations" with people who believe in the school's "vision and values."[104] As ESR, like many other schools, moves forward in an uncertain economy, it may be challenging to keep education affordable. In comparison to other peer seminaries, ESR keeps its tuition fairly low[105] so students who feel called to ministry can reasonably pursue that leading. ESR also offers Cooper Scholarships, which cover between one-half and two-thirds the cost of an ESR education.

---

[104]Jay Marshall, "ESR Seeks Major Gifts to Build Endowment," *Earlhamite* (Winter 2009), 32.

[105]Sulek, *Case for Support,* C–22.

ESR today is nowhere near its financial situation in the 1960s and 1970s, when sometimes faculty did not know from one year to the next whether or not the school would be open. Now that the school is more established, the financial challenges are different with an aging donor base and even less denominational loyalty than in the past.[106] ESR is still committed, though, to preparing Friends leadership in the 21st century and is confident that way will continue to open. This is a matter of faith.

ESR in the World of Friends

After students complete their degree work at ESR, graduation is really just the beginning of living into a life-long call to ministry. Some follow their calling back to ESR, as some former and current faculty and staff members have done; others find themselves ministering in different parts of the world. Benson Khamasi Amugamwa (2008) returned to Tiriki, Kenya and his teaching at Friends Theological College, a school that prepares pastoral leadership among Kenyan Friends. FTC is currently under the interim leadership of Ben Richmond

---

[106]*Self-Study Report for the Association of Theological Schools* (2006), 20.

(1983) and will soon be led by Ann Riggs, a former ESR adjunct professor. Julia Ryberg (2007) continues to reside in Sweden, where she works with the Friends World Committee for Consultation to create electronic community opportunities for European Friends who are at a distance from meeting communities. She has also developed an introductory course in Friends faith and practice and trained Friends from other countries to use the material in their home contexts.

ESR graduates have provided past leadership as yearly meeting clerks, secretaries, or superintendents, such as Sam Caldwell (1979) and Thomas Jeavons (1978) for Philadelphia Yearly Meeting, Frank Massey (1984) for Baltimore Yearly Meeting, and Curt Shaw (1980), Western Yearly Meeting. Others provide current pastoral leadership, including Phil Baisley (1993), Williamsburg Friends Meeting; Stan Banker (1976), Indianapolis First Friends Meeting; Joshua Brown (1984), West Richmond Friends Meeting; Sheldon Clark (1999), White River Friends Meeting; Donne Hayden (2006), Cincinnati Friends Meeting; Frank Massey (1984), Jamestown Friends Meeting, North Carolina; Deborah Seuss (1991), First Friends Meeting in Greensboro, North Carolina; Curt Shaw (1980), New Castle First Friends Meeting; Chris Sitler (2006), Dublin Friends

Meeting; Jackie Speicher (2004), Xenia Friends Meeting; Violeta Tribandiene (2002), Ada Chapel Friends Meeting; April Vanlonden (2004), Fountain City Friends Meeting; Bill Wagoner (1974), Friends Memorial Church in Indianapolis; Jeff Wolfe (2007), Bloomingdale Friends Meeting; Brian Young (2009), Berkeley (CA) Friends Church; and Matthew Zuehlke (2006), Wilmington Friends Meeting.

Other alumni/ae encourage and nurture undergraduates through campus and Quaker ministry. Trayce Peterson (1998), Carol Sexton (2001), and David Hogg (2005) have served on Earlham College campus ministries staff, and Michael Birkel (1979) is Director of the Newlin Center for Quaker Thought and Practice, with Trish Eckert (2009) serving as Assistant Director. The Newlin Center is responsible for Quaker programming, encouraging young Quaker leaders, and representing Quakerism on Earlham's campus. Other ESR alumni/ae nurture Friends leadership at Guilford College through the Friends Center and the Quaker Leadership Scholars Program. Max Carter (1975) and Scott Pierce Coleman (1993) are current staff members there. Sara Beth Terrell (1982) has previously served at the Friends Center, as well.

A number of ESR graduates are or have been involved with Quaker youth and education. Derek Parker (2004) serves part-time as Minister for Youth and Children at Irvington Friends Meeting, and Della Stanley-Green (1990) was for several years on the planning committee for YouthQuake, a Quaker youth gathering that drew attendees from across the Quaker theological spectrum. Ken (1994) and Katharine Jacobsen served Olney Friends School from 1995–1997 and 1999–2003. Ken, as head of school, and Katharine, as a development officer, played a role in helping the school determine its future direction. Maria Crosman (1973) is head of the religion department at George School, and Sheila Langdon Garrett (2001) teaches at the Meeting School in New Hampshire. Eric Mayer (1994) is chair of the religion department at Westtown School.

Chaplaincy is another area to which many ESR graduates feel called. The organization Quakers in Pastoral Care and Counseling was originally an idea put forth by Jesse Paledofsky (1987) that Bill Ratliff "carried forward" in 1990. QPCC is a professional organization for Friends whose faith grounds their work in pastoral care, counseling, chaplaincy, and healing, and QPCC also promotes connection and support for Friends in their field.[107] ESR alumnae Maureen McCarthy (2003), a chaplain at Friends Fellowship Community, and Katherine Jaramillo (2003), a hospital chaplain in Portland, Oregon, are on QPCC's Steering Committee. Other graduates with present or past involvement in chaplaincy work include Victoria Burke (2000), Marie Cavanaugh (2000), Frances Forster (2000), Beth Lawn (2003), Jesse Paledofsky (1987), Jean Semrau (1987), and Jon Shafer (1991). Several recent graduates have completed or are in the process of completing Clinical Pastoral Education units, including Jeff Crim (2005), Mac Lemann (2007), Lisa Lundeen Nagel (2006), Andrea Miotto (2007), and Jacquelynn Shroeder (2005).

ESR graduates also find themselves involved in Friends organizations, both large and small. David Brindle (1980) served as the head of Friends World Committee for Consultation, and Margaret Frazer (1997) is currently executive secretary of the Section of the Americas. Several alumni/ae have worked at Pendle Hill, including William (1966) and Frances Taber, Ken (1994) and Katharine Jacobsen, and Carol Sexton

---

[107]Quakers in Pastoral Care and Counseling, "About QPCC." Available at: *http://www. qpcc.us/7128/index.html* (accessed 5-12-2009); "Annual Conference." Available at: *http://www. qpcc.us/7101/index.html* (accessed 5-12-2009).

(2001). Jackie Speicher (2004) encourages Friends and others to consider simpler living through Right Sharing of World Resources, a small organization located in Richmond, Indiana. Some ESR graduates do work for which they are not paid. Christine Greenland (2002) is a member of the Friends Tract Association, an organization that publishes and distributes literature on Quaker faith, practice, concerns, and history. Lucy Davenport (1993) handles general inquiries for New Foundation Fellowship, an organization particularly dedicated to recovering the Christian faith and vision held by early Friends. New Foundation Fellowship publishes *Foundation Papers*, a small journal that features historical or scriptural essays and personal testimonies written by Friends (often Conservative) from around the world—the United States, the United Kingdom, South America, and eastern Africa.

In addition to the work of alumni/ae around the world, ESR works to support Friends at the Monthly Meeting level. For this reason, ESR offers the Traveling Ministries program, which sends faculty free of charge to monthly meetings or retreats to speak about specific topics, such as the Bible, Quaker faith and practice, congregational growth and management, education, or spirituality. ESR also presents a Vitality series in

Philadelphia, a strong Quaker center in the east. Hosted by monthly meetings and Friends schools, ESR faculty give talks and workshops about vocal ministry, leadership and gift-identification, discernment, and pastoral care within the monthly meeting. ESR also has hosted conversational dinners in Richmond and Carmel, Indiana around specific questions, for example: "What are the most pressing issues as we prepare persons for ministry in the 21st century?", "What message do Friends have to offer the world today?", "What resources do you need for your meeting to succeed?", or "What should be the role or relationship between ESR and yearly meetings?" ESR wants to keep the dialogue going between Friends and the school; ESR can learn what the larger Religious Society of Friends needs, and the larger Society can learn what the school has to offer. ESR and the Religious Society of Friends can check each other's perceptions and understandings through these conversations.

An ESR education—whether that involves a degree program or a single course—is not the end of a journey, but rather preparation for one. Many ESR graduates enter the world of Friends with sharpened skills in teaching, pastoring, campus ministry, chaplaincy, counseling, writing, and cross-cultural ministry, and some graduates simply continue the path they were already traveling, only this time with a greater sense of purpose and empowerment. Other graduates enter a world of ministry with other denominations or organizations. Hopefully all students leave ESR with a deepened sense of their call and gifts for ministry, practice and experience in trying them out, and openness to continue living into God's will for their lives. And hopefully ESR and the larger Religious Society of Friends will continue to enrich and enable each other as they live into God's call for the Religious Society of Friends and its future.

CONCLUSION:

ESR LOOKS AHEAD BY LOOKING WITHIN

Elton Trueblood spoke of the specialized Quaker ministry—specifically pastoral ministry—as a paradox to the universal ministry early Friends deeply felt and believed in. Today
at ESR, pastoral ministry is less of a paradox than it was 50
years ago. None of the current ESR literature speaks of specialized ministry. In fact, current catalogs speak only of universal
ministry, and ESR means no disrespect to Trueblood. Universal
ministry at ESR has come to mean all the types of ministry to
which God can call anyone. Wil Cooper wrote, "ESR holds that
New Testament concept of ministry, which places emphasis on
calling and function rather than position and status." If God

asks someone to speak during meeting, the person's message is ministry; if God calls someone to pastor, then the person carries out pastoral ministry. Likewise, if God calls someone to write, nurture, listen, or teach, then every one of these things is ministry. As a school of religion, ESR recognizes particular types of ministry for which it can best equip the students, but the calling is, and has always been, God's.

For the past 50 years, ESR has been in its own discernment process for ministry. Whom is ESR meant to serve? How should it serve? What can the school do to improve its service? Wil Cooper conducted a feasibility study in 1959 with some of these questions in mind. Over the past 25 years, ESR has continued to ask these questions. In the mid-1990s, ESR revised its mission statement in a major way to direct more outwardly its sense of Quaker identity. The school built on this work by conducting the 1998 consultation among Friends; the Religious Society of Friends spoke, and ESR listened. As a result of that conversation, ESR was empowered to articulate clearly its Christian, Quaker identity, as well as to find ways to live more deeply into that identity. ESR also felt empowered to be a visible presence among Friends, to continue to prepare Friends for leadership and ministry, to be a model of Quaker education and scholarship, and to be a place that fosters spiritual growth and transformation.

ESR often finds itself in the middle of larger Quaker tensions. When Friends struggled with evangelical and liberal theology, so did ESR. When Friends disagreed over what constitutes ministry or worship, ESR felt the disagreement and responded by preparing pastors for programmed Friends and leaders for unprogrammed Friends, which ended up confusing the larger Society. Being in the middle can be uncomfortable place, but it is also a life-giving and fruitful place. Because ESR serves the broad center of Friends, different kinds of Quakers come to the school and learn things they did not know. Some Friends engage the Bible for the first time; others sit in unprogrammed worship for the first time. Some have their first encounter with plain-dressed Friends at ESR, and Conservative Friends meet their first Quaker pastor. Friends from Africa and South America sit at the same table in Common Meal. Non-Friends discern a call for their lives and find the welcoming, spiritual atmosphere helpful to their own spiritual formation.

As ESR enters the next phase of its life, the school faces the reality that the Religious Society of Friends, at least in terms of North American numbers, is in decline. If membership continues to decrease at its current rate, American Friends "would be extinct sometime late in the 21st century," according to one calculation.[108] This is not a particularly pleasant thought, and ESR cannot solve the problem by itself. What ESR can do is be a place that cares about the future of Friends and Friends leadership. Already ESR has hosted a Young Adult Friends conference and published books on Friends vitality. ESR sends faculty, free of charge, to conduct workshops in Friends meetings through the Traveling Ministries program. The school's *ESR Access* program allows Friends to prepare for ministry from a geographic distance. Quakerism in Africa is growing, which makes it all the more important that ESR continue making connections with Friends around the world. Although ESR cannot be all things to everybody, the school wants to be in touch with the global pulse of the Society, to feel and know the heart and mind of Christ in all Friends, no matter where they are, whether in Kenya, Honduras, London, Philadelphia, San Francisco, Newberg, Barnesville, or Richmond.

As Friends understand it, true power and transformation come from within. ESR holds that "Christ is present, guid-

---

[108]Sulek, *Case for Support*, B–12 and B–13.

ing and directing our lives, and we can know and obey Christ's will." This credo, originally articulated by Wil Cooper, has appeared in ESR catalogs since 1960. The statement confesses an inward, but living Christ who has a will and directs our lives. Conservative Friends, the tradition in which Cooper grew up, would recognize the Christ described here. Not accurately described as either evangelical or liberal, these Friends fall somewhere in the middle with Christ-centered, unprogrammed worship. While some Conservative Friends still disagree with Cooper's ideas about ministry preparation and theological education, the Wilburite spiritual influence on ESR may be greater than some Friends realize. ESR's place as a middle ground where Friends can gather owes itself, at least in part, to these quiet Friends whose Christ-rootedness anchors their meetings, their work, and their lives. Cooper was following his Guide when he founded Earlham School of Religion, and 50 years later, ESR has made a difference in the lives of Friends in the United States and around the world. The school recognizes with sadness Wilmer Cooper's passing in 2008 and gives thanks for what the Spirit of Christ has done through him. ESR also looks forward to seeing new ways and paths the school will take in the 21st century.

The Quilt and the Cross

When people enter the ESR building, they often notice the large quilt hanging over the dining room doors. The quilt, made by Emily Cooper in 1995–1996, shows a lion and lamb sitting next to each other against a dark blue night sky with stars and flying doves. Around and above the lion and lamb are numerous different colored circles flowing in and out of each other. The quilt's lower border has a painted text from Isaiah: "The lion and the lamb shall dwell together in peace." Emily Cooper designed the quilt with ESR's Common Meal in mind, specifically thinking of the moment when the community forms a circle and holds hands before the meal begins. Many students and visitors comment on the beautiful, calming colors, as well as the theme. Some think the quilt reflects ESR and the Quaker tradition very well. Peace and circles go together; both give a sense of completion, of wholeness.

Facing the quilt on the opposite wall is another circle. The circular, interior window by the second floor elevator overlooks the Gathering Area below. For many years, the window remained empty. One day in 1998, Emily Cooper paid a visit to Jay Marshall. The lion-and-lamb quilt was attracting too much attention, she said, and made a suggestion. Perhaps ESR could put some other artwork in the Gathering Area, just something else for people to look at. Marshall and Cooper discussed the possibilities and the available locations, and after a while, they decided a sculpture might fit inside the circular window. Marshall contacted McGaws in Boston, Indiana, who brought three sculptures for display in the Gathering Area. For the next few days, the ESR faculty and students gave thoughts and opinions. In the end, most people favored the sculpture called *The Eye of God*, a large cross with amber-flecked blue glass at the juncture of the two beams. Marshall had it installed in the circular window the following year.

The cross provokes interesting discussions. For some, the cross is "too high church" because Friends have not historically had images or symbols in their meeting houses. Others find the cross jarring because it represents something hard to understand: difficult things about themselves, difficult things about God and Christ, difficult things about the Christian tradition. Some others think nothing of it; the cross represents Christian tradition, and what is wrong with that? Still others see the cross and feel a welcoming and inclusive sense of community. The cross and the quilt hang in the same room, facing each other, each its own symbol, each with its own circle of completion. Between these two artworks, ESR students, faculty, staff, and visitors form their own circle for Common Meal and bring together their joys and concerns—all the beautiful and hard things—and commend them to God, who is always present and in the heart's deepest center.

BIBLIOGRAPHY

Published Resources

Among Friends: A consultation with Friends about the condition of Quakers in the U.S. today. Richmond, Indiana: Earlham Press, 1999.

Bill, Brent. "'Not Always Easy, But Good': Five ESR Grads Talk About Pastoral Ministry." *ESR Reports* (Fall 1999), 1–3.

Cooper, Wilmer A. *The ESR Story: A Quaker Dream Come True.* Richmond, IN: Earlham School of Religion, 1985.

Dobyns, Keith. "The PRISM Project." *ESR Reports* (Fall 2001), 4–5.

Grannell, Andrew P. "On Becoming a Friends Center for the Revitalization of Ministry." *ESR Reports* (Fall 1991), 1–2.

Hamm, Thomas D. *Earlham College: a History.* Bloomington, IN: Indiana University Press, 1997.

Hinkley, Scott. "New Building Update." *Nexus* (Fall 1988), 7.

Hisrich, Matt. "Exploring Faith & Economics in Argentina." *ESR Reports* (Fall 2008), 6.

"Jay Marshall Named Dean of ESR," *Quaker Life* (June 1998), 13.

Kawamura, Stacy. "IYM Proposes to Support Anderson Quaker Professor." *Earlham Word*, October 25, 1991.

Kostlevy, William. *Bethany Theological Seminary: A Centennial History*. Richmond, IN: Bethany Theological Seminary and Brethren Journal Association, 2005.

Main, Steve. "Realignment: When Core Values Collide." In *Realignment: Nine Views*

Among Friends. Wallingford, PA: Pendle Hill, Monday Evening Lecture Series (Autumn 1991), 11–16.

Marshall, Jay. "ESR Seeks Major Gifts to Build Endowment." *Earlhamite* (Winter 2009), 32.

Mullen, Tom. "The Dream and the Dreamers." *ESR Reports* (November/December 1990), 1–2.

Mullen, Tom. "Truth in Statistics." *Earlhamite* 97(1), 1976, 12.

"New dean excited to be at Earlham School of Religion." *Palladium-Item*, Richmond, IN: April 25, 1998.

"New ESR building ready for occupancy." *Earlhamite* 109 (Fall 1989), 3.

Punshon, John. "The Work Ahead: Thoughts and Hopes." *ESR Reports* (Fall 1991), 2–3.

Punshon, John. "Quaker Studies at ESR." *ESR Reports* (Spring 1992), 1, 3.

"Purpose Dictates Form of New ESR Building." *ESR Reports* (Spring 1987), 1.

Samuel, Bill. "Realignment Among North American Friends?" Available at: http://www.quakerinfo.com/quakalig.shtml. Accessed 2-17-2009.

Tribandiene, Violeta. "ESR in Lithuania." *ESR Reports* (Fall 2006), 5.

Unpublished Resources

Friends Collection and Archives, Richmond, Indiana:

Andrew Grannell Papers

Earlham Board of Trustees Minutes

Earlham School of Religion Board of Advisors Minutes

Files from the Office of the Earlham President

Indiana Yearly Meeting Executive Committee Minutes

Wilmer Cooper Papers

Earlham School of Religion, Richmond, Indiana:

Cooper, Wilmer and Tom Mullen. Interview with Bill Ratliff. Videorecording, 2002.

Earlham School of Religion ATS Accreditation Self-Study, 1986.

Files from the Office of the Earlham School of Religion Dean

Information from Seminary Academic Services, Office of the
    Registrar

Self-Study Report for Accreditation Review, 1996.

Self-Study Report for the Association of Theological Schools,
    2006.

Sulek, Marty. *Case for Support*, 2005.

INDEX

academic degree, 11, 13, 15,
16, 44, 88, 91, 92, 93, 95,
102, 106, 107, 111, 113,
121, 127
academic education, x, xi, 3, 4,
5, 6, 7, 9, 10, 13, 14, 16, 17,
20, 22, 23, 24, 29, 30, 31,
32, 33, 34, 35, 40, 41, 44,
47, 48, 49, 51, 52, 56, 60,
62, 63, 66, 68, 69, 71, 72,
75, 77, 78, 79, 80, 83, 87,
88, 90, 91, 92, 94, 95, 97,
99, 100, 101, 102, 106, 107,
109, 111, 112, 113, 115,
118, 119, 120, 121, 124,
126, 127, 130, 133
accreditation, 2, 10, 12, 61, 93
admissions, 87
alumni/ae, 10, 16, 29, 31, 32,
33, 44, 81, 85, 92, 96, 97,
109, 110, 113, 114, 119,
122, 123, 124, 125, 126,
127
Among Friends national
consultation, 78, 79, 80, 81,
84, 85, 91, 93, 94, 130, 137
Amugamwa, Benson Khamasi,
102, 121
Anderson School of Theology,
40, 41
Anderson, Paul, 109
Anderson, Peter, 113
Angell, Stephen, 109
Applegate, Judith Middleton,
33
applied theology, ix, 10, 25, 33
Association of Theological
Schools, 2, 12, 29, 48, 87,
88, 91, 108, 116, 118, 121,
140

141

LaVergne, TN USA
23 September 2009
158846LV00001B/11/P